I0459870

Lotus

A Memoir About Resilience and Hope

BY **Xavia Jones**

Edited by Lynda Wheeler
Co-edited by Jean Douglas
Designed by Xavia Jones
Cover Photo by Solomon Kelly Photo

Xavia Jones

Lotus

A Memoir About Resilience and Hope

Published by Fifth Street Publishing Roselle, IL
For permission requests, write to the publisher at:
info@fifthstreetpub.com

Disclaimer

This content is not intended to diagnose, treat, cure, or prevent any mental health or psychological condition. The experiences and reflections shared are those of the author and should not be considered a substitute for professional advice or therapy. Readers are encouraged to seek support from a licensed mental health professional or medical provider for any mental health concerns.
The author's intent is to offer hope, healing, and a sense of connection through shared experience, not to provide clinical guidance.

Trigger Warning:

This book is intended for informational and inspirational purposes only. It contains personal stories that touch on sensitive topics such as trauma, domestic violence, loss, and mental health challenges. Some readers may find these topics emotionally triggering. Please take care of your well-being as you read.

ISBN: 979-8-218-58224-1, 979-8-218-58225-8

Contents

PART 1 - Cracks In The Mirror

Murky Waters 4

Mom 12

Name It & Tame It 19

Chocolate´ 34

Seventeen and Pregnant 42

LL Cool Jay 50

PART 2 - Breaking Points and Quiet Awakenings

Graduation 65

Night Shift 78

Isaiah 86

April Showers 91

Fight Flight Freeze 101

Independence Day 117

PART 3 - The Return with Wisdom

The Safe House 127

New Beginnings 135

Transform and Transcend 148

Part 4 - The Gifts Gathered (MY TOOLBOX)

Coping Skills 157

Mindset Shift 162

Reinventing Yourself 171

Love 174

Know Thyself 177

The Foundation 181

Appreciation 186

Notes 187

Pathways and Resources 190

To The Lotus Foundation INC., a symbol of resilience, transformation, and the undeniable strength of single mothers determined to rise. This book is for the women who refuse to be defined by their past, who fight for their futures, and who bloom despite the heaviness of life. May this foundation be a beacon of hope, a source of empowerment, and a reminder that we all have the power to rewrite our stories.

With love and purpose,
Xavia Jones

A portion of the proceeds from the sale of this book will go toward The Lotus Foundation INC

Foreword

By: Dr. Regina S Brown

As a clinical psychologist, I have worked with persons exposed to all kinds of challenging life circumstances in my 30 years of mental health practice. I have witnessed both the horrific impact of trauma exposure and the remarkable resilience of the human soul despite those wounds. When Xavia approached me to write this foreword, I was honored— not only because of the courage it takes to share such deeply personal experiences but because of the invaluable gift she offers to others walking similar paths.

This book is not just a memoir. It is a roadmap written by someone who has navigated the treacherous terrain of multiple traumas and emerged from hard-fought battles with deeply-rooted wisdom. Xavia presents her story with transparency, sharing honest insights about devastating and disorienting personal experiences. As a Christian woman, she refuses to sanitize the brutal realities of trauma by boldly presenting herself as fully human despite the pressure to do otherwise. She discusses the perfect storm of social, relational and religious roles and their varied expectations and how, in some ways, they perpetuate traumatic and abusive cycles by not providing a roadmap out of them. Xavia's process includes revealing her own mistakes, setbacks and moments of doubt along the way to her remarkable growth and healing. There is a tendency in sharing stories of recovery to fast-track through the pain in an effort to skip to "the good part" while ignoring the struggle, confusion and uncertainty it takes to get there. Thankfully, Xavia does not do that.

What makes this book particularly powerful is its authenticity. There are no false promises of easy recovery or simple solutions. Instead, Xavia offers something far more valuable: the real, messy, nonlinear process of healing presented by someone who has lived it. Her willingness to examine her own choices and acknowledge her own emotional needs is vulnerable and courageous. She does this with grace and not with self-condemnation. She takes accountability while treating herself with compassion that comes from deep personal work. Telling the truth is ugly and scary especially when the outcome is unknown. She had no idea how revealing her experiences will land and yet she did it anyway. It is clear that she has taken hard looks at her own "stuff" to be able to provide readers with this unmasked view of her experiences. Xavia's story provides a model for readers who may feel anchored and stuck in their situations by shame and self-doubt.

In my clinical practice, I often see trauma survivors who feel isolated in their experiences, convinced that no one could truly understand what they have endured. This book serves as a powerful antidote to that isolation. Through her story, Xavia reminds us that survival is not about perfection but rather it is about the cumulative impact of making one decision after another coupled with persistence, self-compassion, grace and the gradual reclamation of one's own life and voice. Readers will find the discussion of practical tools helpful in shifting their mindsets, taking inventory of decision-making, values and relationships particularly valuable in their own transformational processes.

Most importantly, this book demonstrates that our wounds do not need to define us but instead they can inform our purpose. Xavia has transformed her pain into an example of hope for others, proving that survival is not just about enduring. It is evidenced in growing, learning and ultimately using our experiences to light the way for those who follow. I encourage readers to approach this book with open hearts and minds, prepared to be challenged, moved and ultimately inspired by one woman's extraordinary journey from wounded to survivor to thriver.

Part 1

Cracks in the Mirror

What is it about the Lotus?

It's more than just a beautiful flower. One thing about me, is that I am constantly seeking deeper meanings, trying to connect the dots between the things I encounter and the pieces of my life that matter to me the most. I found myself doing that when I decided to get my first tattoo.

I waited until I was thirty-six. It wasn't a spur-of-the-moment decision, it was something I'd been thinking about for years. It started with a conversation I had with a few of my cousins. We all went bowling, just hanging out and catching up with one another. We referred to our time together as, "cousin night out." We grew up in a big family, and we were all pretty close. There was a significant amount of time spent at our grandparents' house. It was there that we learned the roots of our faith and family. Our grandmother was the heart of it all; grounding us in the traditions and values that helped define who we were. Even though she's been gone for years now, we still carry pieces of her with us, trying to honor her memory in our own ways.

As the years passed, staying connected as a family became more important to us, especially after the loss of our matriarch and patriarch. We don't get together as often as we'd like, but when we do, it's as if no time has passed at all. That night at the bowling alley was one of those rare moments, a chance to reminisce, laugh, and share what was on our minds. My cousins had all gotten tattoos long before me, so when the conversation turned to body art, I mentioned that I wanted mine to carry a strong meaning.

Psalm 139:14, "I praise you because I am fearfully and wonderfully made; your works are wonderful…"

The words made an impression, not just with me but with all of them. It wasn't just a powerful affirmation of self-worth; it was a thread that tied us back to our grandmother's teachings. And so, the idea was born, a cousin tattoo —with four of us going on to carry that scripture in our own way. Each of us would take that verse and reimagine it through our own artistic vision.

For me, the vision was clear: a lotus, its petals across my wrist, with the scripture cascading down like a stem. I wanted the tattoo to be more than just a design; I wanted it to symbolize something deeper. So, I did what I always do, I started researching the lotus. I wanted to understand its meaning, its journey, and the story it told.

What I found was nothing short of magical. The lotus begins its life in the darkness of muddy waters, but as it grows, it rises above the surface, stretching toward the light. It is a symbol of strength, resilience, and transformation. A plant that thrives, even in the harshest conditions, I connected with that.

In many ways, the lotus is a perfect metaphor for our lives. It's a reminder that, even when we're surrounded by darkness or struggling through difficult times, there is always the potential for growth, for beauty, for something greater. Just as the lotus pushes through the muck and the mire, we too can rise above our circumstances, embodying strength, renewal, and transformation.

For me, the lotus became a symbol of hope: a promise that no matter what challenges we face, we have the power to overcome and bloom into the fullest version of ourselves. Emerging from darkness into light, finding beauty and strength where I least expected it—that's been my journey. The Lotus isn't just a flower; it's a living testament to what's possible when we refuse to stay stuck in the mud.

Murky Waters

"I'm sorry!" I belted out. My apologies didn't subdue the yelling.

"Why would you do that!?" He kept screaming at me. There was no answer I could give that would satisfy his frustration. My mind just couldn't process why so much fury was directed toward me. In my opinion, leaving an empty bowl on my nightstand wasn't a big deal. I stopped talking, but the yelling continued until I exploded.

"I'm sorry! I'm sorry! What do you want me to say?" I pleaded. But the yelling persisted, and finally, as I was holding my ten-day old baby, I snapped. "Stop yelling at me, dammit!" Before I could finish my outburst, he reacted.

He grabbed me by the throat. His grasp tightened, and I couldn't yell anymore. I couldn't even breathe. "Don't curse in my house," he hissed through his clenched jaw and tight lips, as his grip constricted further. I held on to my baby tightly, terrified I might drop him. We were standing near the stairwell banister, and all I could think about at that moment was keeping my child safe. If he didn't let go soon, I feared I would lose consciousness and drop my son.

Then he released me. I was consumed by rage. I laid my newborn on the bed to make sure he was safe before unleashing my outrage. I knew better than to hit him, but if my words could've been punches, I was ready to give him the ass whooping of a lifetime. I was yelling, crying, and cursing, but he swiftly bear-hugged me. Wrapping his arms around my body, clenching his left arm with the right for a firm grip, he squeezed harder and harder. He buried his chin on my chest, making it impossible for me to move. His grasp was so tight that he squeezed the air from my lungs. There is nothing worse, nothing more helpless, than being unable to breathe. I collapsed with him falling on me. As we hit the floor, I heard a loud crack. The sharp pain in my right ankle confirmed it was broken.

I cried out, asking him "WHY SEAN!!!", but there was no answer. Moments later, the doorbell rang. It was our pastor's wife, a mother figure to us. He went downstairs to greet her. I heard her always pleasant voice saying she was in the neighborhood and wanted to see the new addition to our family.

I wiped my tears and hobbled to the top of the stairs. "I think I need to go to the hospital," I said. "What happened?" She asked concerningly. That moment was my chance to say something, get help. The timing of her unannounced visit was so ironic, but I wasn't ready.

I had to put on a brave face. It was almost instinctual for me to perform. It didn't take much for me to assume my role; adapt to the performance. I chuckled, "Oh I didn't see Joe's toy on the floor," I said as I quickly made up a lie about being clumsy and tripping over something. Without hesitation I lied to protect him, to protect the image of my perfect family. She agreed to stay with the kids while we went to the urgent care facility around the corner.

At the urgent care, I lied to the nurse, saying I had tripped while walking backward. It actually made no sense. Sean sat there while the nurse asked, "Do you feel safe at home?" She was going through the routine questions that were meant to detect abuse. I guess she couldn't read my body language or catch my version of the Morse code I was blinking, "Help me." Looking back, I wish someone had pressed harder. But I also believed what Sean had told me, that it was my fault for going "crazy," and he was just trying to calm me down.

This wasn't the first time he'd been violent, but this incident was different. I thought he had changed. We had gone three years without any physical violence, but what I didn't recognize is that he didn't have to be physically violent anymore. The emotional abuse was enough to keep me bound to this toxic cycle. Still, I was just grateful he wasn't hitting me anymore. After that day, he never let me out of his sight. With four kids, a high school diploma, with a nursing assistant certification, I felt trapped. So, I suppressed my feelings and carried on. It took me two more years after that day to finally decide that

I was done. It wasn't easy, but I became open to the idea that I deserved more, seeking something better for myself and my children. Finding my way to a life that was less limiting than the life I was living.

My ex-husband was a harsh man, full of explosive anger. More often than not, his reaction was disproportionate to the situation. It reminds me of that scene in The Avengers where Captain America calls Bruce Banner, saying, "Dr. Banner, now might be a really good time to get angry." Banner turns and reveals his secret, "I'm always angry." I used to call my ex the Hulk, not because of his stature, but because he had a constant, unbridled anger lying dormant, ready to erupt at the smallest trigger.

I lived in a constant state of inadequacy and fear. Every misstep was magnified, every unmet expectation—met with punishment. There were also moments of charm and charisma. He was either hot or cold. I lived for the good times, the laughter and the security of being taken care of by someone who, I thought, loved me. Yet, the looming fear of his next eruption always cast a shadow over those moments.

The tiny joys of life were often stolen moments I found . One of my small delights was eating butter pecan ice cream, a brief escape from the chaos of raising four kids: a newborn, a toddler in diapers, another potty training, and a rambunctious six-year-old. Breastfeeding was my only moment of rest, my time to enjoy something for myself. That day, he was angry that I left the bowl on the nightstand.

Sean had taken some time off work to help with the other kids, and he was usually kinder to me after I gave birth. However, I was always in tune with his moods, adapting to his disposition and assuming responsibility for managing his anger. My codependency had me convinced that the stress of having four children was setting him off, when in truth, he never needed a valid excuse to fly off the handle. That day, I tried to stay calm as he badgered me about the empty ice cream bowl. We had just moved into a beautiful townhouse, only ten minutes from my parents. I was thrilled to be close to my mom. Sean was stressed, but I was stressed too.

After the birth of each of my children, I fought postpartum depression, with my last child being the greatest struggle. I had learned to recognize the signs by then, but this was more than just baby blues. It was fear, anxiety, restlessness, and thoughts that didn't feel like my own, robbing me of the joy of motherhood. After my first child, I was connected with a hospital program for new moms, where a case manager visited weekly, offering literature and support. This was my first point of education about postpartum depression, which I had never heard about until I became a mother, but it would haunt me for years thereafter.

Our marriage was tumultuous in a lot of ways, but we maintained a facade. I was the director of the children's ministry, and he was involved in the church too. We projected the ideal Christian marriage, a submissive wife and a God-fearing husband. We hid behind religion, which only perpetuated the toxicity.

It wasn't until I found a new church and connected with an incredible mentor that my life began to change. She exuded peace and confidence, something I longed for. She was one of the few people I was able to connect with. I made sure to keep in touch. I often called to check in with her, and during one of our check-ins, she was telling me how she felt blessed and how her life felt fulfilled. Her words lit a fire in me, and I realized I couldn't maintain the facade any longer. I wanted to be able to say that my life was fulfilled. I didn't really know what that meant but I knew that it gave me a goal to strive toward. I needed to know what being fulfilled meant for me.

Therapy was a strong force that helped examine the condition of my mental state. Talking about the abuse, the infidelity, and my feelings of helplessness forced me to confront the truth. I did not realize how deep I was consumed by the feeling of despair until I began to open up. It was through therapy that I broke the seal that I used to suppress my emotions. Realizing that what I thought was protecting me, was actually suffocating my ability to live freely.

I started taking small steps toward my independence; getting a job at a hospital, building my credit, saving money, and reading books that helped me overcome my feelings of worthlessness. The fear began to dissipate as I took control of my life.

Sean tried to escalate his control, but I was no longer afraid. Eventually, I left. I went to work one day and didn't go back home. I felt like I had nowhere to go. I was homeless. At the time I was working a part-time nightshift at a hospital as a patient care technician. I had no money with just the clothes on my back, which were the scrubs I wore to work. It didn't bother me. I tried to leave before but didn't want to give up the security of my lifestyle. I also dreaded the idea of being a single mother. That thought process kept me bound to a fantasy life, however, in reality I had to bury the essence of who I really was to bear the truth of a severely broken marriage. I hit a breaking point, and everything was different. At that time, my peace was worth more to me than anything, more than a beautiful home or any other synthetic version of happiness. I decided to stop letting someone determine I was not worthy of love, respect, dignity, or empathy. That someone was me.

My ex-husband wasn't responsible for my self-worth nor my happiness. It took me years of personal work to realize that. Back then, I was in an emotional prison trapped by my own feelings of self-loathing, shame, and guilt. He manifested outwardly the inner narrative I kept telling myself. My hope is that by sharing my story, someone else can use it as a point of reference on their path to freedom.

As my mentor once said, "You are the author of your life. If you don't like the chapter, write a new one." That's exactly what I did. I decided that my next chapter would be a story written from a place of healing, forgiveness, and hope—relentless hope.

The truth is, we are far more than the sum of what has happened to us. Our pasts do not dictate our futures. Every struggle, every setback, every moment of pain and hardship is not a life sentence, but rather a lesson, a point of reference for how far we've come and how much we've grown. My past doesn't determine who I am meant to become; it serves as a testament to my resilience, my ability to rise, and the grace that has carried me through even the darkest times.

I've come to realize that the life I desire is not something I must wait for, or hope will be handed to me. It's something I am capable of creating. I am in control of my future, and so are you. When we stop letting life merely happen to us and instead choose to participate in it, we discover that we have the power to rewrite the story. The life we envision is not a distant dream; it is something we are worthy of, something within our reach.

The narrative of my life is no longer shaped by what others have done to me or what circumstances I have had to overcome. It is shaped by my decision to rise above, to embrace my purpose, and to live with intention. Every step forward, no matter how small, is a step toward the life I was always meant to live. It's not about where I've been, but where I'm going. My story, just like yours, is still unfolding, and we hold the pen.

Mom

My mom had me when she was twenty-two. At that tender age most young adults are exploring all that world has to offer, while attempting to curate their identity and decide the direction of their future. She was on track to finish nursing school but stopped when I came along. For the most part, it was just the two of us. My mom was the middle child in a family of 14 children, but she never acted like a typical middle child, fighting for attention. Instead, she was shy and quite unassertive; a subtle force who rarely raised her voice, except when it came to Jesus.

My mom's love for the Lord was unshakeable. Growing up in a Pentecostal household with a strict upringing, she wrestled with the legalism of religion but always sought her own relationship with God. Over time, she came to realize that loving the Lord wasn't about rigid rules, it was about grace. Eventually, she found the freedom to wear pants without feeling condemned. She proudly proclaimed her faith everywhere, even when I, as a kid, found it a little embarrassing. She carried gospel tracts wherever she went,those little folded pieces of paper with scriptures in red ink and the Lord's Prayer of Salvation on the back. Every human interaction was an opportunity for her to bring someone closer to Christ. When men would approach her, thinking they were smooth, she'd simply ask, "Are you saved?" That was usually enough to send them on their way.

We spent a lot of time at church. She led some of the youth programs, so of course, I was right there with her. I didn't mind going to church, it was so ingrained in me as the way of life. We went to a non-denominational church, which was very different from the churches my granny took us to. As a timid kid, I didn't quite fit in with the other kids at church. Plus, my mom always dressed me like I was five years old, and I hated it. The socks with the frilly tops were cute when I was two, but as I got older, I really despised going to church, mostly because my mom picked out church clothes. I would catch the glance and hear the snickering from the other kids. I was sure they were all making fun of my extremely conservative dresses while they came to church pretty casual.. I never had the heart to tell my mom I didn't like the clothes.

Back in the '90s, my mom was a model. I grew up watching her walk the runway at local fashion shows alongside her best friend, Gina. I loved spending time with Gina. I thought she was one of the prettiest women I ever saw. She didn't have any children so she treated me like one of her favorite nieces. I was fascinated with her Creole accent and wavy hair. I wanted to be just like her and my mom when I grew up. I admired my mom's beauty, grace, and humility. She was a beauty and had a figure that drew attention. She moved as if she did know how much attention she allured, especially from men.I didn't quite understand the passing gazes as a kid. It just sort of annoyed me. I felt like I needed to protect her in some way. She didn't play into the attention too much from what I could tell. Her focus was on surviving and raising me.

Even though things seemed great from my point of view. Just me and my mom. She wanted more. She desired to have a husband. As a twenty-something year old woman she felt like that was the next step in life.

My mom never married my biological dad. I remember her first husband being this very tall and handsome man. His name was Maurice. He had a very charming and outgoing personality, much like my father. It made sense. My mom was meek and mild-mannered, so she attracted the opposite. I remember playing with his twin daughters. They lived next door to my grandma Jones' house on Chestnut, the east side of Rockford, Illinois. They didn't date long before we moved to Colorado. My mom was young and didn't want to struggle as a single mother. Getting married probably felt like a way out of struggle and a ticket out of Rockford for my mom.

Whether my mom knew before we moved to Denver or not, her husband had a violent and reckless temper. Everything about him scared me, and I never trusted him. His unpredictable impulsive behavior was something that could take a dangerous turn—let me tell you what I mean. There was a time we took a day trip to the mountains and it turned into something traumatic for me and my mom. We drove up the mountains and as we stood gazing over the city, he picked me up, held me over the mountain cliff, quickly let go, and then grabbed me again, laughing hysterically. My mom panicked, and he didn't seem to understand what the big deal was. I never saw them enjoying one another. I don't remember my mom being happy with him at all. I do remember him being angry. Angry enough to throw a small TV at my mom during an argument.

My mom ultimately left the abusive marriage, and it was just the two of us again, in Colorado trying to make it. I was happy that it was me and my mom, side-by-side.

Always seeing violence play out in most relationships I saw as a child, created this subconscious norm that these things just happen in relationships. That didn't stop me from being afraid. In fact, the fear became ingrained in my understanding of love and companionship. Even as a child, I knew something wasn't right, but when violence is normalized, it becomes easy to convince yourself that it's just part of life. According to the National Coalition Against Domestic Violence (NCADV), 1 in 15 children are exposed to intimate partner violence each year, and 90% of these children are eyewitnesses to the violence.

The psychological impact of witnessing domestic violence as a child is profound. The normalization of abuse can distort a child's understanding of healthy relationships, creating a cycle that continues into adulthood. Children who witness domestic violence are at a much higher risk of experiencing or perpetrating violence in their future relationships.

Witnessing domestic violence as a child also leads to a range of emotional, cognitive, and social issues. Studies have shown that children who are exposed to violence are more likely to experience anxiety, depression, and behavioral issues. I remember constantly feeling on edge, never fully able to relax, and always bracing myself for the next argument or act of aggression from the adults I was around. It felt like walking on eggshells became second nature, a survival skill in a world where conflict seemed inevitable.

For years, I carried that fear with me into adulthood, struggling to break free from the subconscious patterns that had been ingrained in me during my childhood. I still have a difficult time with people being angry. My entire nervous system reacts. It is one of those trauma responses that takes significant time and effort to create new responses.

My mom's husband eventually wanted her back, and I was terrified that she would go. He invited us to dinner sometime after my mom left him; I was nervous. I didn't want to go back. As we sat at the table, he attempted to ease my mother's agitation by giving me a gift. He gifted me a ring. The ring had my birthstone, a pink tourmaline stone in a gold setting. I felt so many emotions that I couldn't understand. I left the table to go to the bathroom. I locked myself in a stall and began weeping. "I want my dad," I cried. A feeling that followed me for years. It was a helpless sadness, a desire to be rescued. I slammed my head in my hand against the bathroom stall door. The ring bent, smashing my finger into the flimsy aluminum. It was cheap. The ring was cheap, just like his apology to my mom. I immediately stopped crying and shifted to fear. Did I break it? I quickly squeezed it back into shape. Then, I headed back to the dinner table.

After her divorce my mom felt the impact of once again, doing it alone—as a single mother. My mom struggled, and she had hoped my father would help her financially, but he didn't. I was too young to understand how much my mom was trying to survive, but I felt it. One morning we left out of our apartment to rush me to school only to find the car was not there. It had been repossessed. At the time, I didn't think of it as a negative experience. I just enjoyed the fact that my mom and I spent time together walking everywhere as she held my hand while we trudged through the snow. I treasured those kind of moments —when I felt close to my mom. She called me her pumkinita, and she was my world.

I remember being terrified that something would happen to her. When she would put me to bed at night I'd try to tie my hand around her nightgown, so I'd know if she tried to leave in the middle of the night. I would twirl my hand around and around the satin fabric—gripping as tightly as I could. It never worked. I would wake up from nightmares of her being hurt to find she had escaped my makeshift tether.

I took on this responsibility to protect her emotionally—the kind of protection that kids can adapt to as a sense of love and loyalty. I suppose, as a kid, I didn't have the ability to identify it but perhaps, I sensed the exhaustion from the weight that she carried. So, I felt as though if was "good" I wouldn't cause more stress.

Colorado was nothing but bad memories, and eventually, we returned to Rockford. Despite everything, I was happy to go back to what I knew, back to family.

Name It & Tame It

Back in Illinois my mom and I lived in this small, cornfield-filled city just about 30 minutes from my grandma's house. Belvidere is a farming town in Illinois—a rural city with roots in manufacturing. The nearest major city is the fifth largest in Illinois—Rockford. Even though the two were neighboring cities, the communities were extremely different. Belvidere provided a small town atmosphere while Rockford has maintained having one of the highest crime rates in the nation. Although the cities were close, they seemed hundreds of miles apart. Living in Belvidere allowed my mom to be a bit removed from Rockford, the city where she grew up and where I was born. Though we lived just on the outskirts, everything and everyone we knew was on the southeast side of the city. Some parts of Rockford didn't have the best reputation. Drugs, crime, and gang violence have plagued the area for the past few decades. The 1990s marked the height of the surge. The Southeast Side, in particular, was far from a picture of opportunity and prosperity. Crack cocaine ravaged the city, giving rise to drug houses in many neighborhoods. Daily gang shootouts became a grim norm throughout the city.

One Fourth of July, me and my cousins stood in front of my grandparents' house waiting for the fireworks, when we saw an old Chevy cruising slowly down the block. Something felt off. The car stopped in the middle of the street. Then, the headlights cut off. Without saying a word to each other, we all instinctively ran to the porch, nearly tripping over each other and ducking.

POP! POP! POP! Shots rang out.

We never knew exactly what happened that night, but moments like that were just a part of life on South 5th Street. There were so many times things could've gone terribly wrong, and one of us kids could've caught a stray bullet, like so many others had. We loved being together as a family, but we couldn't ignore the reality of our surroundings.

It felt like the city had a way of holding people back, making it hard to better yourself if you stayed there. My grandparents' house was right in the center of the chaos. We all grew up together in that big black-and-white house on the corner of South 5th Street and 8th Avenue. Granny and Pops raised fourteen children there, and hundreds of grandchildren passed through. When the family first moved to South 5th Street, it was a beautiful, safe neighborhood. After the next generation came through, the area changed drastically. The house next door was a crack house, and the one across the street had prostitutes coming and going all day. Dope boys, boosters, and hypes were always around, but they all seemed to respect my granny. From my naïve child's perspective, it didn't seem all that bad. One of the area's biggest dope dealers came by and brought my granny food and other goods that were probably stolen, but she'd share whatever it was with all of us. He seemed like a nice guy—showing up with diapers and even fresh fish sometimes. Random people like that would often stop by to see one of my uncles who lived at my grandparents' home. "Mother Walston" is what everyone called my granny.

There was a prostitute, Cherry, who frequently visited my grandma to ask for prayer. I can still hear her say, "Wrench over there and hand me my bible." My granny wouldn't hesitate to pray for anyone. Cherry would even bring her pimp sometimes. Granny seemed like she was always praying. In fact, she prayed so much we didn't know when the conversation smoothly went from talking to praying. Once you realized that she had switched to prayer, we'd quickly bow our heads, close our eyes, and agree, "Yes, Lord," ever so often. Minutes felt like hours, but those prayers were comforting.

Granny never looked you in the eye, but she always knew what was going on. She had a sixth sense about things. You would always find her posted up in the corner of the dining room in her Lazy Boy, next to an open bible, watching Robert Tilton, one of the famous televangelists from the 90's. You might even catch her watching WWF—she had a thing for Stone Cold Steve Austin. The only time she'd leave the house was to go to church or to the rare doctor's visit, but the house was always full. We always celebrated the holidays together. My grandparents' home was always packed on Christmas and Thanksgiving. Even if there were no holiday festivities going on, my granny was always cooking, so whoever stopped by could go into the kitchen and get a plate.

Since I was my mother's only child back then, my cousins were the closest thing to siblings I had. I still like to brag that I was probably the only grandchild who never got whooped by Granny back then. I learned my lesson by watching the others. Granny was a steadfast Pentecostal; she could pray fire down from heaven, and if that didn't convict you, she wasn't shy about using bodily harm. I never knew what it felt like to be hit with a switch, but when Granny sent us out to pick one for someone else's whooping, I learned how to pick the right kind. I'd always choose a dried-out branch that broke easily because I hated seeing others get hurt.

As everyone got older, the whoopings turned into fights and threats of serious harm. There's an urban legend in the family that my granny knocked my uncle's eye out of his head with a broomstick. So, when my granny threatened to knock our eyes out of our heads if we rolled them when we had an attitude—we believed her. That one uncle didn't come around much, but whenever I did see him, I'd stare to see if he really had a prosthetic eye.

Abuse and domestic violence were normalized parts of my childhood. At times the chaos outside my grandparents' house paled in comparison to the dysfunction on the inside. Violence was how disagreements were handled, and sexual abuse was swept under the rug. At times I was more afraid of what went on inside the house than anything happening in the neighborhood.

Some of my uncles and cousins got sucked into the fast life of money, gangs, and violence. One of my aunts was tougher than all of my uncles combined. She was a major player in the dope game back in the day. I saw my uncles, older cousins, and even my aunt in and out of jail. We often celebrated when they returned home after doing time.

Celebrating when my family members came home from jail was a bit layered. On the surface, it was just about love and the relief of seeing someone you cared about regain their freedom. We celebrated as if it were the biggest victory because, in many ways, it was. In those moments, the fact that they had survived the system and made it back to us felt like something huge. We would get together at my grandparents' house, embrace them like they had been gone for years, (sometimes they had been) and laugh through the difficult time.

The family came together in those moments, not just to celebrate their return, but to remind them that they were still loved and still a part of something. For many of us, it wasn't just about them coming home, it was a small taste of victory in a life that often felt like we were losing. Freedom, in that context, was something major we all wanted to hold onto, and celebrating it made us feel, even if just for a moment, that everything was going to be okay.

Underneath the joy and love was also the realization that the bar was set incredibly low. We were celebrating their return from being locked up or sent to boot camp, not from achieving something great or life-changing. Those places had already robbed them of so much. Looking back, I realize the bittersweetness of those moments. Our standards for success and safety were so skewed by our circumstances that freedom itself became the ultimate goal.

The love was real, but so was the underlying recognition that we were celebrating their survival, not their thriving. The expectation was simply to make it out alive and not get caught up in the system again. The low bar was set by the world we lived in, a world where staying out of jail felt like the highest form of success. We weren't talking about dreams, ambition, or personal growth. We were just grateful they came home in one piece. That was the reality we lived with, and it was a reality shaped by a system designed to see us fail.

During those celebrations, you could see the potential for something more, love, family, resilience, but also the sadness that we were forced to accept survival as the victory. It was hard for us to see it in the moment, but now I understand that while we celebrated freedom, we were also grappling with a system that had lowered our expectations so much that freedom itself felt like the only thing worth hoping for.

With freedom being the goal, that environment automatically taught us to be vigilant about danger and recognizing our limits. I remember running up and down the block on South 5th Street, knowing not to go too far because just around the corner was a house with two rottweilers ready to jump the dilapidated chain link fence. I had to be about seven when I saw the barrel of a gun pointed at my face. There was this guy, maybe about sixteen; I thought he was one of my older cousin's friends. He was walking down the street, this white kid with a buzz cut and baggy jeans, was moving like he had somewhere he had to be—quick. I noticed a gun hanging out of his back pocket. In my curiosity, I asked, "Is that real?" He pulled the gun out, put it in my face, and asked, "You want to find out?" Terrified, I said "no" and bolted back to my grandparents' side of the block. That environment taught me to keep my head down, to not ask questions about the things I saw, because asking too many questions could get you hurt. It taught me that expectations were limited to just staying alive, staying out of jail, or making it through another day without getting caught up in something worse. The love in our family was strong, but so were the invisible fences keeping us from imagining a future beyond just surviving.

My grandfather, Pops, was always present, but as kids, we didn't understand that he was a functioning alcoholic. Our grandparent's home was deeply matriarchal, and though I don't recall ever having a real conversation with Pops, we were constantly around him. We'd help him build things in the garage, crush cans for him to recycle, and even paint the white fence that surrounded the house, but our favorite moments were watching him make his famous homemade ice cream.

Despite his limited education—he couldn't read and never made it past the third grade—he knew how to count his money and play dominoes. With 14 children to provide for, Pops worked relentlessly, whether out of necessity or simply to escape the chaos at home. He spent decades working at one of Rockford's oldest manufacturing companies, Gunite. Even a damaging work accident didn't slow him down. In fact, he was once fired from his job at the junkyard—not for neglecting his duties, but for working too much.

Most nights, he came home stumbling and incoherent. The severity of his state would sometimes dictate how volatile the night would become between him and Granny. If she managed to get him into the basement, she'd lock the door behind him with a bolt lock. My cousins and I witnessed their fights often, convinced that one day they might kill each other.

My grandpa brought a gun home after days of fighting with my granny. I don't know if he actually planned on using it, but he certainly threatened to shoot my granny. My mom had to go into the basement where he lived, away from everyone else, to convince him to get rid of the gun. My granny was never afraid. She actually dared anyone to try her. That was her house, and she ruled with an iron fist. She kept a butcher knife by her side and waved it around during arguments with Grandpa, my uncle Billy, or anyone else who dared to cross her.

I became detached from the violence, witnessing it so much. My uncles were violent toward their girlfriends, and my aunts were abused by their husbands. What I learned from all of it was to stay out of the way and avoid being noticed. My silence worked; I was never hit. However, my extremely withdrawn demeanor did make me a target for other things.

Why didn't I speak up about the things that were happening to me and around me?

Much later in life, my therapist and I were working through some of my childhood experiences. What he told me was how the body reacts to the trauma, much like a self-preservation response. To regurgitate what happened would mean reliving the pain. Our bodies do not want to experience pain. That is when a child can shut down and retreat inward, keeping things tucked away. I lost my ability to speak and to advocate for myself early in life. My ability to recognize my agency did not exist in my childhood.

My mom wanted to protect me from all the dysfunction, but as a single parent working full-time and sometimes an added part-time jobs—she often had no choice but to leave me with Granny, Pops, my aunts, uncles, and cousins. Even when my mom even moved us to Colorado, trying to escape Rockford, she brought the dysfunction with her and ended up in an abusive marriage.

Like Granny, my mom didn't spank me much. She always said I was a mild-mannered child. On the rare occasion that she did, it was an entire process. First, she'd explain what I did wrong, then she'd pull out the Bible and read the verse about sparing the rod and spoiling the child. She'd always remind me of her unease by saying, "This hurts me more than it hurts you." I actually believed her, and I hated to make her upset.

Outside of my cousins, I had a best friend whose mom, Pam, was my mom's childhood friend. Our families were close, and their house, outside of my family, was the only place I was allowed to spend the night. Pam had a big personality, always smiling, always talking, a complete contrast to my mom's quiet demeanor. One Saturday morning, after a sleepover, her daughter and I were told to clean the bathroom. Apparently, we weren't doing a good job, because we were called into the room for a whooping. I wasn't cleaning the floor right, she told me. I walked into her daughter's bedroom. The lights were off, and the daylight peaked through the windows. I obeyed when she told me to turn around and put my hands on the bed. She had a wooden bunk bed. I leaned over and placed my hands on the lower bunk. To this day, I have a scar on my right butt cheek from being beaten with a PVC pipe. When my mom came to pick me up, Pam sat her down in the room where I got my first real beating. Pam listed everything she thought was wrong with me. Not just that I was lazy, but every little thing about me that annoyed her. She told my mom that I pretended like I was allergic to shrimp so I didn't have to eat it.

My mom sat on the bed, sort of withdrawn with her body language. Her head was down as Pam was talking. She had a meek spirit; never reactive no matter the situation. Looking back my mom had to be overwhelmed by Pam's overbearing explanation because my mom didn't respond right away. I wasn't sure how to take that. At that moment, my soul confirmed that I was fundamentally flawed.

That experience gave root to my inner critic that "something is wrong with you," and "you deserve being punished." Clearly, I had deserved what happened to me. That was the message that I received as a little girl. My mom never let me go back to Pam's. Years later, we heard that Pam had spiraled into a battle with bipolar disorder, losing her family and ending up homeless and on drugs. My stepdad even saw her at the crack house next door to my grandparents' house. But after years of struggling, she got the help she needed. I reconnected with my childhood friend, and she shared the painful timeline of when she essentially lost her mother to mental health issues. Thankfully, she was able to mend her relationship with her mom. I also had a chance to talk with Pam as an adult. Over a call, she tearfully shared her regretful actions that led to her losing my mother as a friend.

Back then, nobody talked about mental health. We saw my uncle Billy go in and out of the local mental health facility, but no one ever discussed why. We just thought he was "crazy." In the '90s, that's how some people with mental health issues were labeled. There was no understanding—no real support.

My uncle David was diagnosed with schizophrenia. It was a long battle that drove him to take his own life. Mental illness surrounded me, but no one had a true understanding of it.

Looking back, I realize Pam wasn't just scolding me that day ,she was critiquing my mom's parenting. Later my mom explained that she didn't know the extent of the beating I had. It was hard for her to process what happened. She wrestled with the idea of Pam being her best friend and knowing how to respond to the situation. Pam whooped me for all the times that my mom didn't. That was the beating of a lifetime—literally. It took me years to learn how to find my voice and advocate for myself. We can only build from what we have.

The road to finding my voice meant that I had to release ownership of what happened to me and allow the ownership to rest with the adults responsible for protecting me. I choose not to hold resentment, but to view the experience with empathy. Empathy for a young mother wrestling with trusting people with her child. Empathy for a woman battling with mental illness. Most importantly, I had empathy for a little girl who was worth being protected.

The groundwork of who we are is developed very early in life. This is where the pathways of familiarity are developed.

These pathways connect our life experiences to what we cognitively resonate with from our past. My upbringing directly impacted how I saw myself in the world and in my relationships. I was exposed to violence throughout my childhood. Whether I realized it or not, dysfunction and violence were familiar to me. Unintentionally, I found my way back to what was familiar as I ventured out into the world, trying to find my place in it.

When we acknowledge the story of our lives, we give ourselves the opportunity to connect to the emotions behind those experiences. Identifying those pivotal moments and capturing the feelings associated with them allows us to gain a deeper understanding of ourselves. While these emotions are a crucial part of self-discovery, they don't have to take root in the fabric of our identity. They can shape the way we navigate life, but they don't have to define us or be carried forever.

For much of my life, I learned to disconnect from my environment as a means of survival. It was a skill I unknowingly mastered. I chose to shut down my emotions and withdrew when things became too chaotic or unsafe. Those survival mechanisms didn't stay neatly tucked away. They began showing up in other areas of my life. I would withdraw emotionally in situations that required me to be assertive or open. Recognizing this about myself was both humbling and freeing.

My therapist calls this process "name it to tame it." It's the idea that before you can change how you show up, you have to acknowledge the disconnect between the person you want to be and how you're currently responding to life. Naming it means going back to the source of the disconnect and acknowledging where those survival skills came from, and how they served you. For me, naming it meant admitting that my ability to emotionally detach as a child was a way of protecting myself in a world that didn't feel safe.

Survival skills don't belong in the environments that you've cultivated to be safe. Once you name those patterns, you can tame them. Taming it might look like reshaping the narrative you've told yourself about that emotion, changing how you respond to it, or even altering how it manifests in your body. For example, I've learned to sit with uncomfortable feelings rather than push them away. It's not easy. Even with the strongest attempts, those feelings don't entirely disappear. But they don't have to control how you show up.

This process is uncomfortable, like sifting through the recesses of your mind to unearth memories you'd rather leave buried. But if you want to approach life, love, or relationships in a more intentional and authentic way, it's worth the effort. Pain doesn't just vanish, it lingers, subtly influencing how you respond to life. By doing the work to name it and tame it, you give yourself the power to respond to life on your own terms, not from a place of survival, but from a place of growth and choice.

Chocolatè

When we first moved back to Illinois from Colorado, we lived with my grandparents. My grandparent's house was the hub for anyone in the family who needed a place to stay. I believe my grandmother delighted in being a refuge for the cruelty life brought. There was a revolving door that constantly spun. Aunts, and uncles, cousins, rotated the three bedrooms that were upstairs. I never remember seeing an empty room, regardless of who was moving out. Eventually, my mom was approved for Section 8 housing and we moved out of my grandparent's home.

Section 8 vouchers were a lifeline for low-income families, offering a chance to live in better neighborhoods and secure stable housing. My mom eventually found a two-bedroom apartment in Belvidere, in a newly developed complex surrounded by cornfields. I never knew that we lived on government assistance. My mom made sure I never felt like we were without.

In 1994, Belvidere had a large Hispanic community, and at the time, I felt like the only black kid in my entire elementary school. Desperate to fit in, I quickly gravitated toward my Hispanic peers. I learned to dress and talk like them, of course, the first thing I picked up were the bad words in Spanish. More than anything, I wanted to blend in, to feel like I belonged.

The daily reminder that I didn't belong echoed loudly as the kids chanted, "Chocolatè! Chocolatè! Chocolatè!" whenever I got on the bus. I had dark skin, and to them, I was different. I stood out. One kid in particular, Carlos, seemed to have a special hatred for me. He wasn't satisfied with just calling me "Chocolatè." He took it a step further and started calling me "Mayatè," apparently Spanish for the N-word. It was more than just teasing; it was his way of making sure I knew that, in his eyes, I was beneath them. Being different fed into my already mounting sense of shame.

It wasn't just the Hispanic kids reminding me of my place in this predominantly white and Hispanic town. The white people in the neighborhood also made sure I felt out of place. I had issues with those kids too. After having a confrontation with one of the boys at the bus stop, their dad decided to come and stand with them one morning. The dad yelled out at me as I got on the bus, "Make sure you sit in the back of the bus, you n-." The words stung, and for a brief moment, I felt like I had been transported back in time to the Jim Crow era. This middle-aged white man had no shame in hurling racial slurs at a 10-year-old girl. I wrestled with an inner conflict. On one hand, the back of the bus was where all the cool kids sat, and I wanted to sit there, too. But on the other hand, I didn't want him to think I was sitting there because of his racist demand. As the bus pulled away, I shot him a defiant middle finger from the back of the bus, knowing full well I was making my own choice, not because he told me where I belonged.

Fitting in at school became a constant battle. I had to develop thick skin, especially around the boys like Carlos and his gang of friends.

One day, I ran into one of his minions, Ricardo, in the hallway. We had words, typical kid stuff, but this time, I wasn't backing down. He called me "pinche mayatè," and I shot back a comment about his ridiculous rat-tail, a 90s hair fashion I found laughable. We were on the verge of a fight when a teacher stepped in. He grabbed both of us by the arm and placed my melanated skin next to Ricardo's sun-kissed brown skin. "Look, you are the same," he said. At that moment, it hit me. Here we were, two minority kids fighting over who was "more minority. "The teacher's words broke the tension. After that, Ricardo and I never had another issue.

Eventually, I was accepted by my peers. My grade school best friend was a Hispanic girl who taught me all I needed to know about the culture. I eventually didn't see myself as different, and decided to embrace the different cultures that I grew up around. During that time, I was taught the skill of adaptability and accepting change. A skill that followed me, providing opportunities to connect with all kinds of people from different cultural backgrounds.

Although we lived in Belvidere, I spent a lot of time in Rockford with my extended family. That all changed when my mom married my stepdad. He was different from anyone I had seen my mom with before. To this day, I've never seen them argue. He adores my mom and always has. He made sure she knew it. He brought her flowers and constantly told her she was beautiful. Their relationship made me feel safe in a way I hadn't experienced before. It wasn't just about the words; he showed his love through actions. It gave me a sense of security knowing that my mom was with someone who truly cared for her. This was my first example of a healthy relationship. They had a mutual respect for each other in a way that demonstrated a healthy partnership.

I was with them all the time. What I didn't realize was that they were taking me on all their dates. Me and my mom were a package deal, and it seemed as though he understood that. We went on adventures visiting downtown Chicago. We walked along the paths that separated the city from Lake Michigan and found shaded areas to have picnics while throwing around a football. Coming from a small town, those adventures were a big deal. My stepdad was just as intentional about building a relationship with me as he was with my mom. That level of consistency and emotional safety created a bond between me and my stepdad. I trusted him and leaned on him for those feelings of connection and family.

Not long after they married, I got the little brother and sister I had always wanted. I remember asking my mom for a sibling so many times, often with tears in my eyes. Being an only child had been lonely at times, and I longed for the bond that only siblings could bring. When my sister was born, I was eleven, and it felt like my heart expanded overnight. With her arrival, and later my little brother, we truly became a family.

When my stepdad made a point to build a relationship, not just with my mom, but also with me, he became my best friend. We played video games together. He made sure I had the latest sneakers, and he even taught me to play basketball. In the summers, I would wake up before sunrise and drive with my stepdad to Chicago in his work van. It was an old brown van filled with cookies and other dry foods he distributed all over the city. We would pull up to the warehouse, and I would help him load the boxes into the van. I never complained about the tough physical labor or the early mornings. I actually enjoyed spending time with him. I watched him closely as he conducted business: talking to the managers of the grocery stores we visited, laughing and making jokes. It was in those moments that I got a front-row seat to how men conducted themselves as they took care of business, and made deals. To this day, I joke about how I was my stepdad's first son. He wasn't delicate with me. He got married and suddenly had a nine-year old. He only knew how to be a man, so he taught me the parts of life that traditionally were masculine skills. He taught me my strong work ethic in a way that was extremely hands on. We'd open the giant boxes of products and put them on the shelves at the stores. "You have to make sure the new products go behind the products that are already on the shelves." He was very rigid and meticulous. He made me understand the importance of presentation and product placement. He would point out how sloppy the Pepsi guy put up his end cap display and teach me every detail of his efficiency.

As I grew older, I realized my stepdad wasn't just teaching me how to stack cookies or load a van, he was teaching me the value of having integrity, work ethic, and commitment. These lessons would later become the foundation of how I approached life. He gave me a strong sense of a determination that I don't know if he realized would have such an impact on my life.

My stepdad's hard work got him a job at a major food distributor and moved us to the Chicagoland area. Our lives changed drastically. We left my mom's Section 8 apartment in Belvidere and moved to a luxury apartment thirty-five minutes from downtown Chicago just in time for me to start junior high. It was a completely different world from what I was used to. One of my closest cousins, Nicole, came to help us move. She stayed for the summer, and that helped me adjust to the neighborhood. Once school started, I had to find my own way in a new school in what felt like a completely different world. I was navigating yet another new chapter in life.

Trying to find a sense of belonging doesn't end in childhood, but it certainly starts there. It is the foundation of finding a sense of identity that happens in the formative years. At different points later in life, you find yourself needing to connect with others, and you start to create spaces where you feel seen, valued, and safe. Childhood adaptability can show us that belonging isn't just about being accepted, it's about knowing that you matter to the people around you. That creates a sense of belonging and connection that stays with you throughout your life.

Consider a flower with its roots below the surface of the ground, connecting itself deep into the soil. The roots use the soil for nutrients enabling it to grow. If that flower is uprooted from its environment and placed in another, pieces of the roots are left behind and a new system of rooting begins to take place. The flower itself does not change, it continues to grow in the new soil.

Belonging, I think, is a lot like that flower. Sometimes, we're forced to uproot ourselves, whether it's through new relationships, unexpected changes, or simply time. We leave behind what we knew and are faced with the challenge of finding connection again. In those moments, we learn that belonging isn't tied to a specific place or even a specific group of people. It's something we build through the willingess to be open and intentional.

As we move through life, the need for belonging doesn't disappear, it simply evolves. The lessons we learn as children, such as: love is shown through actions, respect creates safety, and that inclusion fosters connection, those are the roots of the relationships we build.

Belonging isn't something we find; it's something we develop over time. And just like that uprooted flower, the process might look different for everyone, but the goal is the same, create a life where we feel grounded, no matter where we are.

Seventeen and Pregnant

Leaving Belvidere, where I felt like the only black kid in my school and even my neighborhood, was a culture shock. I slightly resented having to also leave my extended family but looked forward to having a new beginning. I had to adjust to my new life in the suburbs. Going to school in the suburbs of Chicago felt like I was thrust into a melting pot of all different kinds of kids from various backgrounds. I found myself able to adapt and find life-long friends. I spent a lot of time with new friends, and their families became mine. We moved to the Northwest suburbs to a town called Rolling Meadows. It was far enough from Rockford and close enough to Chicago to feel like we moved to a big city. When I did go back to Rockford, my cousins got a kick out telling their friends I was from Chicago. That was fine and all until I came across someone who was actually familiar with the inner city. When they would ask what neighborhood I was from or what side of town, I struggled to admit the truth. At first, I lied and said it was the south side because I didn't know much about the area yet.

I got used to living in the suburbs and grew distant from my family. We didn't visit as much, and they didn't drive to our home much either. Soon, I became less attached to the things that tied me to Rockford.

One of the girls who lived in my new apartment complex became a close friend. Her name was April. I found myself at April's home quite a bit, and our moms were buddies. I would always hang out at her house, that is, if we weren't outside walking around the neighborhood doing absolutely nothing. I knew April had two brothers; her older brother, Nigga-Moose, as he was called around the neighborhood, and her younger brother Matt. Their Mom was single, raising the three of them on her own. April never talked about her dad much, but her mom always kept family pictures on the refrigerator. I happened to notice a picture of another brother April didn't talk about. He was her father's son. Every now and then, I'd ask her about her mysterious older brother. His picture was displayed on the freezer door along with the others. He lived in Texas, where he went to college. I thought he was so handsome. I would tease her about him from time to time, "Tell your brother I said, hey!" He came home one summer to visit, and my curiosity came to a head.

At fifteen, I wouldn't really say I was boy-crazy, but I did have a deep desire to be loved and accepted, and I only needed to find that one person to validate that desire. My first boyfriend was a kid I met in middle school. He played basketball, and at the time, I was on the dance team. I had this "Love and Basketball" fantasy about a high school romance with a basketball player. I wasn't exactly allowed to date, so my parents thought we were friends. Being two broke teens living in different towns didn't make for a long-lasting relationship, so my interest shifted.

I met April's brother and I couldn't care less about high school boys. The first day I met him, I hesitated to go into April's house knowing he was there. I walked in and saw him sitting on the couch with his freshly braided cornrows. "Aren't you going to say hi to my friend?" April asked her brother. "She walked into the room. She's supposed to speak first when walk into a room." He didn't smile; it was just a matter of fact with him. No one ever told me that rule. I immediately tried to fix the awkwardness. "Hey!" I jumped to respond. "Wassup" was all I got initially. His apathetic demeanor intrigued me for some reason. I got comfortable and he started talking to me. I couldn't hide the fact that I was crushing hard.

My friend told me that her brother had a girlfriend back in Texas who he was going to propose to the summer I met him. I don't think April was too happy with the idea that her brother and I liked each other, but it didn't stop her from setting up a time for us to hook up. I think she admired him and just wanted to make him happy. So, he and I snuck around when he was home from college. There were times when he'd entertain me and my friends without his little sister. Eventually, we started our own relationship. That summer, he showed me the time of my life.

The first night he convinced me to sneak out, I climbed out of my bedroom window. We drove to his cousin's place, and then we cruised the streets around 11 o'clock. It seemed like the perfect night. He held my hand in between shifting the gears in his Honda Civic while listening to Ginuwine's, "Differences." He looked at me as he sang the lyrics. This kind of attention was something that felt exciting. I felt grown; thinking, this is the TV romance I wanted. The sort of risky love affair that had me hooked.

We spent a lot of time together over that summer. We even kept in touch once he went back to Texas. I eventually stopped communicating with his sister. Especially, after she moved away from the neighborhood.

My parents moved again after my sophomore year of high school, which had me starting my junior year as the new girl at a school I had no interest in attending. My mom and stepdad bought their first home in a town twenty minutes from where we used to live. Even though I still very tied to my crew in Rolling Meadows, I tried to make new friends. I didn't realize it at the time, but moving from city to city gave me the skills of adaptability. Because I was a very reclusive child, my mom had a habit of speaking for me and forcing me to be friends with people. As much as I hated it, it sometimes worked. She found another black family on our new block, and there I made lifelong friends who would end up feeling like family.

While I was getting used to my new school and new friends, I was more focused on my budding long-distance relationship. I sent letters to Texas, and he wrote back. I called him every chance I got. Although, it didn't take long for me to realize that we couldn't be a thing. I couldn't hide him from my parents forever, and a long-distance relationship wasn't going to work for a girl in high school. That is until he came back to Illinois right around my seventeenth birthday. I don't remember why he was back home in October, but I was thrilled. He picked me up from school in his white, two-door Honda Civic. You couldn't get any cooler than that. My college boyfriend was picking me up from school. I was in love in all the capacities of which I understood love to be, which was very, very superficial.

I felt like everyone would have an issue with me dating my friend's older brother so, in my 16 year old genius-ness - I called my boyfriend by his middle name so that my parents didn't know I was dating my friend's older brother. At one point, we decided he should meet my parents. My stepfather was completely against me dating a twenty-one-year-old man as a seventeen-year-old. I guess my mom had a soft spot for him since she had a crush on my stepfather when she was just fifteen years old. My stepfather was also older than my mom, so she empathized with my relationship. Back in the day my stepdad was the manager at a Rockford grocery store when my mom got her first job. They dated as she got older, but my mom eventually met my dad and had me. My stepdad always reminds me that he bought me diapers when I was a baby, way before I actually knew who he was.

My mom and stepdad had rules for us once they accepted our relationship. I don't know how my twenty-one-year-old boyfriend felt as a young adult, but I imagine it was awkward to date a high schooler with strict parents. We obeyed the rules by all outward appearances, but I found ways to sneak out of the house and skip school just to be with him.

It was November when we had this great idea to go downstate to visit his cousin, who was in prison. I thought I had my alibi straight, but my mother's intuition trumped my not-so-clever tactics. I snuck out of my bedroom window the night before. I got up before everyone else, so no one saw me in the mornings before school anyway. I told my mom the day before that I'd be staying after school. I gave myself plenty of time, I thought. I will never forget the look on my mother's face when I came through the door the evening I had snuck down state.

The look of terror, anger, and disbelief will be permanently stained in my memory. When I walked into the house, all the lights were off. It was a gloomy fall day, so it started to get dark early. When I saw her come down the stairs, I acted like nothing had happened. "Where were you?" She asked. I tried to keep my lie straight, but my friend who worked in the attendance office at school, the one who was supposed to cover for me, had already told her the whole truth. Eventually, I confessed to jumping out of my bedroom window on the second floor the night before. My mom was relieved yet angry and disappointed. That very same day my stepdad called a meeting with my boyfriend. We all met at the Burger King by our house.

My stepdad has always been rigid about the peace in his home. Any time I caused a disruption to that peace, he'd do his best to extract the problem. There was a time when he literally chased boys away from our home. I was sitting in my room one night when he ran after these kids from my school with a bat after they came knocking at my bedroom window. If it were up to my stepdad there wouldn't have ever been any boys allowed—at all. He even told one of my good guy friends that he could never see me again as consequence for him taking me to Chicago. Me and Lil Dub were deep into the city, and we got lost on the south side. He wanted to take me on my first train ride on the L to meet his boyfriend. We were out too late, and my stepdad drove to the city to pick me up. I didn't see Lil Dub again until we were adults.

When my stepdad called that meeting at Burger King he had the same intention—extract the problem. We sat at the restaurant, and my stepdad told my boyfriend how he betrayed his trust and that he could never see me again. As we left the restaurant, my mom looked at my boyfriend as we all walked out of the door and said, "Look at her; she looks pregnant." We went home, and she had me take a pregnancy test that night.

My mother sat on my bed with me as I cried and said, "I'm so stupid," over and over again. I had my life planned. I was going to go to college in Atlanta, to either Clark, or Spelman with my best friend, Tamia. I knew at the age of 16, that I'd study psychology and excel in my career. Teenage pregnancy was not even conceptual, in my mind. The reality of my reckless behavior hit me; I hated myself. I suppose I had that invincibility complex that comes with the lack of brain development as a teenager. I figured I hadn't gotten pregnant thus far, so it wasn't going to happen to me.

My mom didn't grow up in a household where warm embraces were the norm, so physical touch wasn't how she showed her affection. She expressed her love through her kind spirit which was always comforting. Just like when my mom felt the need to discipline me when I was younger. She sat me down, read a scripture from the bible, and never forgot to remind me, "This hurts me more than it hurts you." I believed her then, and I still felt her comforting spirit when we saw the positive pregnancy test. She reassured me that I was not stupid, and things were going to be okay. Now, my stepdad, on the other hand, didn't speak to me for months. My mother knew that I'd need a father during this time, so she reached out to my biological father: "You're going to be a grandfather," she told him.

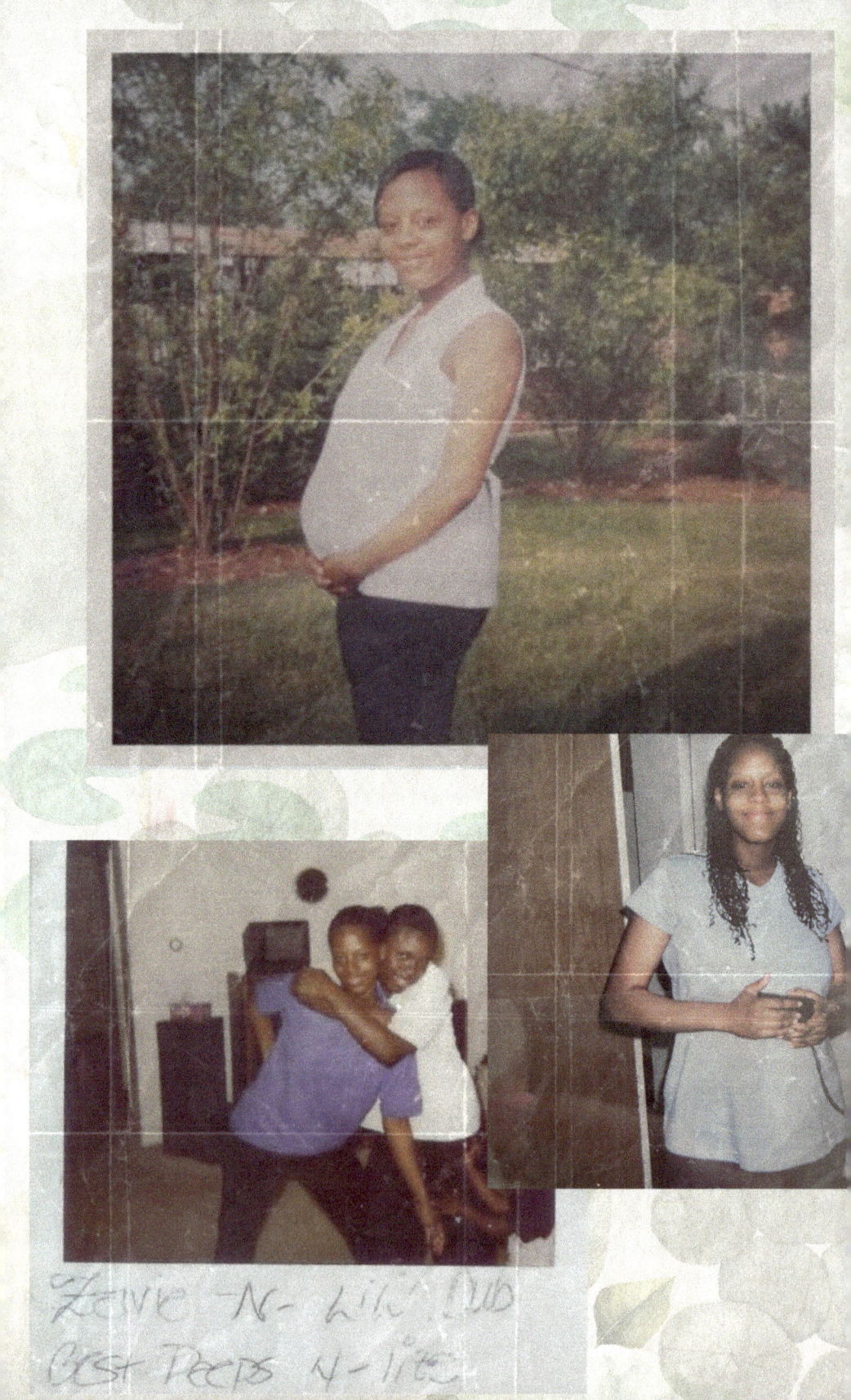

Love -N- Lik Dub
Best Peeps 4-life

LL Cool Jay

My fatherhad this undeniable swag. A kind of charisma that you couldn't help but notice. Even his walk had its own personality. He was a high-stepper, strutting like George Jefferson from The Jeffersons. Tall with a wide step, his arms would sway behind him, keeping rhythm with each stride. As a kid, I found myself slightly embarrassed by how extra he seemed, but deep down, I thought he was cool. EJ had a personality that was infectious, drawing people to him. His laugh was loud and boisterous, filling any room he walked into. And if you didn't notice him at first glance, he made sure you knew he was there. He greeted everyone, always starting conversations with strangers. He had this confidence I had never seen in my entire life. I'm not saying that just because he was my dad. He had this unashamed, larger-than-life personality. He was never afraid to speak his truth and he knew how intelligent he was. His nickname was Jay Bird. My mom told me the ladies loved Jay bird—he was a bit of a ladies man.

I got all my affectionate tendencies from my dad. He was always doting on me with love and attention when I was with him. The way he was meticulous about all the details of me, my clothes, my hair—making sure I was put together, was his love language. He made me feel special; I was his only child after all. I was a daddy's girl in every sense.

I don't remember my parents being together, but I remember having a recurring dream when I was a child. In the dream, I would be standing in front of a door with a stained-glass window. There was always this orange glow that shined through every time I had the dream. The beaming sun through the window seemed to have me mesmerized. It was the focal point of this dream. At times, I would be next to suitcases. Other times when I had the dream there would be yelling in the background, but I was always staring at the stained-glass window in the door.

Years later, my mom would talk about the short period when

she and my father lived together. She would talk about the house my father had on the other side of South 5th St., not too far from my grandparents' home. She told me about the house having a stained-glass window at the front door. That's when I realized that my dream was actually a memory—the only memory I have of them sharing a life together.

We moved to Colorado when I was five. The pain of being away from my father initiated feelings of longing and loneliness. It wasn't long after we moved to Colorado that my mom's husband showed his other side. He was often very angry and seem to have a drinking problem. With my mom being in an abusive marriage, I constantly felt the sadness of being away from the people I loved. My father would call and talk to me every now and then. I knew he really didn't care for my mom's husband. He would ask how my mom's husband was treating me. Eventually, the calls came less and less. Then, I stopped hearing from him all together. I always missed him, even now, I wrestle with the feelings of wanting to have my father around. It feels like I lived my entire life missing my dad.

My mom took a leave of absence from her job at Blue Cross Blue Shield, and we went back to Rockford to visit our family. At some point, my mom decided that we weren't going back to Denver, Colorado, and we stayed in Illinois. When we were back in Rockford, I reconnected with my father, and we spent a lot of time together. He would pick me up from school, and we'd hang out; he'd help me with my homework, and I'd spend time with my stepmom and her son. Jayda, my father's wife, looked just like the singer, Sade. She was kind, and we always had a good time together. One of my favorite things to do was watch Martin with my dad and stepmom. We would stop by the store to get BBQ kettle-cooked chips, then come back home and watch TV.

Initially, when we got back to Illinois, my mom wasn't happy with my father for refusing to help with my needs while she was struggling to make it. She didn't appreciate him showing up at my Grandmother's house and taking me whenever he felt like coming. Since we lived with my grandparents for a while, Granny was the gatekeeper. When my father would show up unannounced, she turned him away at times. There was a point when my father came by to see me, but my Grandmother wouldn't let me go with him. He was extremely upset. My dad was a passionate man, so when he was upset, it was a scene. However, my Grandmother was not to be played with, and she made sure everyone knew that. I was furious with Granny.

All I ever wanted was to be with my dad, but she didn't allow it. I didn't cry; I was just mad. Now, I have never caught a beating from Granny, but to this day, I wish she had just gotten the belt because her words hurt more than any whooping. I sat in the chair closest to the doorway separating the living room from the dining room, slouched in the cushion, arms folded, with pouting lips. Granny looked over to see the disgruntled look on my face. That kind of sass was not tolerated. "You gone cut yo eyes at me! I was the one who saved you when yo momma wanted to abort you! Take yo ass upstairs, Zabier!" She snapped at me. My nickname was Zavy. No one in my family called me, Xavia. My granny's heavy Alabama accent replaced the "v" with a "b" and you got "Zaby," a nickname reserved only for my granny and my uncle Bill. When she really wanted to make sure I heard her, she called me Zavier —with a "b." She rarely was upset with me before then and not much after that. However, those words cut deep. "My mom didn't want me," I thought to myself. I was too young to understand the complexity of that kind of choice being made by a young pregnant woman. Hearing about that initial rejection, ended up nestling right into my subconscious ideas of self-worth.

My mom never spoke bad about my dad to me when I was young. In fact, I don't remember her saying much about him at all. At some point, my father and I were able to get into a consistent flow of visitation, which became a bit easier when we moved to Belvidere. When my mom and stepdad got married things changed. I suppose, with a man being in the home at that time, there was order that had to be established. By then, I was just about 10 years old. My father had to be a bit more organized in terms of co-parenting. He couldn't smoke cigarettes around me, and he had to drop me off on time during the week. He wasn't allowed to take me to R-rated movies—which I didn't like at all. The cigarettes, understandable, but the movies, I felt, was a little too far. I saw all the classic movies back then, like *Mo Money* with my dad. My mom would've never allowed me to see it since it had way too many curse words and violence. I don't think my father cared too much about having rules and guidelines for visiting me. He gave some pushback, but we were able to find ways to enjoy our time together—trying to make the most of our visits.

I knew that my dad loved me. What I didn't know was that he struggled with the downward gravitational pull of living in Rockford. Even though he loved me, I wasn't exempt from the cliché scenario of waiting, in vain, for my dad to pick me up. Looking out my bedroom window facing the parking lot from our second floor apartment; I sat there hoping I'd see the headlights of his car pull into one of the parking spaces. For whatever reason, one day, he decided not to visit. I waited and waited, but he didn't come; and for seven years, he didn't show up, he didn't call, and I didn't get any letters. During that time my mom did allow me to visit my dad's mother. She would take me shopping and give me money and say, "This is from your dad." I'm not sure I believed her, but I loved spending time with, Grandma Jones. Grandma Jones, Mrs. Eloise Jones, was a classy lady. A poised and pragmatic type of woman. My father was her baby boy and they had a close relationship. She was the tether that kept me connected to my father when he was not in my life. At some point he moved away from Rockford. I didn't know where he lived initially. Eventually, my grandmother told me he moved to Minnesota, but that's all I knew.

I remember the first time I did an internet search for my father. I was a freshman in high school when we got our home computer. I couldn't wait to look up my father's name on AOL's search engine. I looked for Edward Jones in Rockford, then in Minnesota, to see if I could find him. You could imagine how many men there were with that name. I never called any of the numbers I did find since I wasn't sure it belonged to my dad. I had so many questions... *Did he have a computer too? Was he looking for me? Does he know where I live? Does he wonder if I am okay?* Ultimately, my longing and sadness turned to anger and frustration. I figured if I could look for him, why didn't he look for me, and why didn't he come to find me? I would have emotional outbursts with my mom and especially my stepdad. I told him one day, in my teenage fury, that he didn't like me because he didn't like my dad. I carried so much anger toward all the adults in my life. Around that time, my stepdad took me for a walk around the apartment complex to have a heart-to-heart about my father. He explained to me why he and my mother broke up. It had to do with my father doing drugs and my mom not wanting anything to do with it. That was the first I had heard anything negative about my dad. I thought he was the greatest human, up until he left with no explanation. I didn't know about his struggles, but it made sense. I got pieces of information about why he left and moved to Minnesota.

My deep-abiding admiration turned into a deep-abiding hatred for my father. The anger helped me cope with the sadness. It was an exchange of pain. It didn't subdue the longing, though. Anytime I felt like life was too much for me, that resounding feeling of, "I want my dad" always resonated. When my mom got in touch with him to let him know that he was going to have his first grandchild, the impressionable little girl in me was super excited at the opportunity to speak to my father. However, I was an emotionally driven teenager, and I had already eulogized my relationship with my father, therefore I had grievances to air. He sent me a cell phone because my stepdad made it clear that he didn't want him calling his house. My Nokia came in the mail, and I was happy to have a cell phone. I was looking forward to talking to my dad. It was a mixture of emotions. I wanted to have a relationship with him, but I had many unresolved feelings. Feelings of abandonment and rejection. Feelings about why he never reached out. We had a lot to talk about.

"Yo, X!" That's what my dad called me. He was the one who named me Xavia. He was so excited to speak to me. His enthusiasm was void of any sense of awareness. He didn't recognize that I had those extreme feelings of abandonment and profound resentment. He had this completely oblivious demeanor as to how his absence affected me. It almost made me feel bad. As he was talking, I remember thinking, this guy has no clue that I have so much anger toward him. He said, he had prayed for the day he could see me. As if I were held captive in another country, he felt like there was this great force obstructing his parental rights. He said that his wife would console him and say, "Just wait until she's eighteen, she'll come back to you." He spent a good amount of time trying to reassure me that he always loved me.

I never understood how bad the co-parenting, or lack thereof, really got. "I am not culpable. Do you know what culpable means?" My dad would tell me that his absence was not his fault. He spent the next few years trying to explain how my mom and stepdad prevented him from seeing me. He tried to tell me about the downfall of his relationship with my mom. He tried to explain that he never left me. He expected me to run to his open arms with the same love and excitement I had when I was nine years old. I couldn't. I was about to have a child, so parenting became very real to me. I could not imagine going years without seeing or talking to my child. Especially since my dad and I had such a close bond.

My dad continued to try to get me to understand, but he was only met with disdain. His love and enthusiasm turned to frustration and emotional distance. He didn't know how to have a teenage daughter. He also had a hard time accepting responsibility for not being around. He couldn't gather how I managed to get myself pregnant in high school. "Was the sex that good?" He asked—trying to figure out what reason I would have to get myself in this predicament. He had no filter. He said exactly what was on his mind with no regard as to how it came across. Because he was blunt and held nothing back, we bumped heads a lot. He didn't know me at all. Here I am, seventeen and pregnant, and all he could gather was that his only daughter was a promiscuous young lady. He might have even used the word, "hoe." Never mind the fact that his absence left an incredible deficit in my self worth.

My desire to have my dad around, to be loved and accepted, landed me in a situation that essentially robbed me of what was left of my childhood. I had no concept of what love truly was. I just wanted the connection I lacked from not having my father in my life and present. For a broken teenage girl, connection meant sex. I confused lust with love. What I needed from my father, I looked to find in a lost young man.

It was difficult for me to build a relationship with my dad. I had a hard time letting him father me as a young lady, since he'd failed to do so when I needed him at the most critical times as a girl. He felt entitled to a certain level of respect that I didn't have for him. My father wasn't easily persuaded to adopt different perspectives. He always felt that I should change how I viewed things, mainly how I should hold my mom and stepfather responsible for his decision to move away and wait until I was an adult to have a relationship. As challenging as it was, I was still grateful to have my father. We found a way to move past those obscure seven years and instead we built a friendship. My father came to admire me as a young woman over the years as we got to know each other. I visited him in Minnesota, and he came to Illinois a few times. The first time I saw him, it was at my grandma Jones' house. As I left that evening, he followed me to the gas station and made sure I had a full tank of gas before I got on the road to drive an hour back to the suburbs. I cried nearly the entire ride back. I was flooded with so many emotions. I wanted dad my dad in my life. I needed him to do dad stuff, like fill my tank up with gas and encourage me when I was going through difficult times.

My father and my stepmom built a life in Minnesota. He left Rockford to find better opportunities, which he did. He worked in IT and really loved the work he did. When I went to visit him with my son, he was incredibly proud. He took me to his job at a hospital in Minneapolis and introduced me to everyone. We went around the city and, of course, to see the Mall of America. It was an amazing time to be with my father again.

EJ had survived prostate cancer. His wife also had a battle with cancer that she didn't win. While he was doing what he could to hold on to his wife, our relationship took a hit.

My father owed my mother back pay in child support, and the state of Illinois made sure he paid. He was furious. For some reason he expected me to advocate for his relief, but I hated being put in the middle. "If you saw a child on the playground being beaten by another child, and you did nothing to intervene, you too are culpable." There was that word again. My father always liked to show that he was very intelligent when he was upset. I find myself doing the same even now. I get really dignified when I want to get the point across, that was him. Looking back, I can understand that he may have been dealing with the fear of losing his wife and may have had a financial burden that came with healthcare costs. I expressed that I never wanted to get involved, but despite my attempt to maintain neutrality, the guilt of not helping my father nestled in my consciousness.

As a young adult, I gave my mom and stepfather some of the responsibility for the fractured relationship I had with my father. But they were there. They made sure I was clothed and ate. They were at my basketball games and provided all the support I needed. How could I have held on to anger toward the people who were actively taking care of me? The best thing for me to do was keep my opinions to myself and maintain the relationship I had with both parents. But my dad's wife was dying. I had to say something. "I struggled when we lived in

Colorado! I asked your father for help. Do you know what he told me? 'You have to eat, don't you? Buy a chicken and give her a leg.'" My mother was highly offended that I would fix my mouth to ask for mercy on behalf of my father. I understood. I carried the hurt of both my parents. Eventually, my mother felt the "Christian" thing to do would be to go to the state and ask to stop the payments. She did.

Eventually, we reconnected again. Once Jayda passed away, he really worked to find his new normal. We talked often, and I was able to visit him in Minnesota again. There was so much I wanted to know about my father. I was searching for a better understanding of who I was.

In 2009, my father's cancer came back. It had metastasized to his pancreas. Before he was diagnosed, he went on a road trip to visit family, and he eventually made his way to me. It was like he knew what was coming. At the same time that year, my mom was diagnosed with a cancerous tumor in her nasal cavity. My father ended up in the hospital during his treatment. At the very same time my mother had to be hospitalized because her body became so weak that she couldn't handle the chemotherapy. I had this terrifying fear that I was going to lose both of my parents at the same time. My dad didn't fear death. At least, he didn't let me see that he was scared. He told me, "We all will have our day. You either go out by getting sick or in a tragic accident. This is my fate."

My parents spoke while my father was in the hospital. I knew that my father loved my mother. A love that lasted a lifetime. When I visited my father in Minnesota I brought a stack of pictures for him to see. As he shuffled through the photos he took a long pause when he reached a picture of my mom. After a deep sigh, he said, "oh, well," and continued to shuffle through the stack. I imagine his apathetic "oh well" was his way of jolting his mind back into the present, refusing to travel down memory lane. My mother had the opportunity to say goodbye. "You know you still love me," Those were his last words to her.

As my dad was given his prognosis of weeks to live, I had to have one last conversation about why he left me. "Dad, if you could do things differently, would you have?" Before he left my life again, I needed to know. I thought maybe thinking about his mortality would prompt him to reflect on his life and maybe soften his perspective. "What do you mean? When I left? I didn't leave you, but yes I would've handled things differently." He gave me the reassurance I needed. The little girl in me just needed to know that my dad loved me. That he would have fought for me. I couldn't make it to Minnesota to see him when he was struggling through his last days to live. I got a call from the hospital one night. It was my aunt. She called to tell me to say my goodbyes.

My dad was ready to cross over. She put the phone to his ear. "I love you dad." He could no longer talk but I heard his breathing increase with intensity. I started telling him how my boys were doing okay. I told him, "I'm going to be okay, dad."

We spent seven years working through the seven years he was absent. His final words to me gave me the peace I needed to release that hurt I carried for so many years. I think about the wisdom my father gave me during that time; you know, the things dads try to teach their children. I will never forget some of the insight and encouragement he shared. My father truly admired the woman I came to be. Every child wants their parents to be proud of them, and he was. He often reminded me that I had the perceptiveness of someone ten years older than me, and because of that wisdom, our relationship was built on the mutual respect that we had for one another.

Part 2

Breaking Points and Quiet Awakenings

The transition between adolescent and adulthood is one of the most defining time periods in a person's life. This is where you are positioning yourself to secure your future; a delicate balance between planning what's ahead for your life or risk derailing from the plan all together. For most, this a space where they are approaching self discovery while preparing for career aspirations. For some teen moms, that can seem out of reach.

How do you have time for self-discovery when you now have someone else to consider? How can career aspirations be at the forefront when affording daycare forces you to take what's available to you, and you end up working hard just to provide. Teen moms fail to get a high school diploma at a rate of 50%. But how do you balance being a mom, getting an education, all while trying to grow up yourself? The likelihood of obtaining post secondary education or training is very limited. This all leads to poverty, struggle, and a lack of the ability to create an environment for the child to achieve success as well.

Graduation

There was very little interest in making friends at this new school on my part. I was there because I had to be. Even though I tried to ingratiate myself into making friends—I felt above the petty high school drama. After all, my boyfriend was in college. I went to school and stayed to myself. I made one close friend who is still my closest friend today.

Another friend I had was a 17-year-old young man who aspired to be a pastor. He had such a kind disposition. I remember being in Spanish class, and he asked if I wanted to go to prom. I told him that I wasn't going to go to prom. I thought about how I would look in a prom dress with a baby bump. The idea seemed completely ridiculous. The shame wouldn't allow me to enjoy my last year of high school. One day, he asked me why my sweatshirt was bulging out. "Are you pregnant?" He asked me this in front of my class. My Spanish teacher heard the conversation and pulled me outside the classroom and whispered to me, "Are you pregnant?" I told her I was. Being pregnant made me feel incredibly ashamed. I tried to hide it for as long as I could. Soon spring rolled around, and it became harder to hide my growing belly with hoodies and baggy sweatpants. I would take the long way to my history class to avoid the girls congregating in the lunchroom during passing periods. Eventually, I would have to face the music with everyone.

Another classroom disruption erupted. A teacher embarrassed me for sleeping in class, I had to be honest about what was happening in my life. "Xavia!" My precalculus teacher had the nerve to interrupt my late morning nap. "Do you want me to send you to the dean's office?" He snapped at me in the middle of his lesson. I countered with a defensive response, "Are you asking me or telling me?" I closed my book getting ready to pack up and head to the office. I don't think he knew how to respond to my nonchalant attitude. I got out of going to the dean's office, but he did hold me back after class. Just a simple question like, what's going on? triggered an onslaught of uncontrollable tears. I let him know why I was so tired in between the snot and tears. "Oh," his pudgy jaws dropped as he realized the reason behind my apathy for his class. "My sister is pregnant too. She's always very emotional. I get it." He mansplained how he made the connection between my pregnancy and the disconnect to precalculus.

As time went on there was no hiding it. I eventually took the short cut to history class, spoke to the girls in the cafeteria, and let them rub my baby bump every now and then. I got the maternity jeans and kept working hard to finish all my classes. I went to summer school, every year, after 8th grade, So, I had just about enough of the requirements to graduate my junior year of high school. I finished my last high school class in July, and I gave birth to my son in August.

Every August Chicago has a celebration to kick off the school year. I loved when my step-dad took us to the south side to watch the Bud Billiken parade. I laid in the hospital bed August 9th 2002 watching the parade on TV. In a way, a piece of me mourned the innocence of standing on the side of the road excitedly watching the parade floats roll by as the drill teams danced down the street. In a few short hours I was going to be a mother. My best friend and my mom were in the delivery room with me. Sean was still in Texas. He was trying to finish his paralegal course before the baby came. I had a picture of him next to me on the bedside table as I prepared to push. He had sent the pictures to me in one of the letters he wrote. We'd correspond back and forth frequently. He once sent me a mixtape with all the best R&B songs. It was something I sat in my room and listened to for hours. He'd send poems. I'd write lengthy love letters. It fit right into the hopeless romanticism of a fantasy relationship.

I kept the letters over the years. Initially, I held on to the words written on those pages as a reminder of the love that we shared. As the years went by, the meaning changed. Now, I keep them for my children. If they ever decide to read them, they will know that at some point, they were created with love in mind.

I realize he and I had never spent a lot of time in each other's space. We met, conceived a child, and maintained a relationship over the phone while he lived in Texas. I was so caught up in the idea of having someone, that I didn't see how we were in no position to start a family. We didn't know each other very well at all, and truthfully, we didn't know ourselves.

3-11-02

I've never felt for any girl the way I feel for you
I'm hoping forever can become reality, so please say "I do".
The thought of us growing as one, sends a chill throughout my body
But what's really exciting is having kids, calling us mommy & daddy.

The odds are stacked against us & there are those who'd love to see us fail
But as long as there's breath in my body, I won't let them prevail
By now you should know that my love will forever remain constant
And I won't run from my responsibility, now that it has happened.

I know me being away can become frustrating but if you can just hold out
I'll treat you better, so that's good. In a couple weeks we
One day will know if it is going to be Mya or Demetrius.
Then I'll also by the end of this week I'll get those last
_____ . I want to say thanx for the money
that you send, it does help. I also wanted to tell
you thankyou for your words of incouragement that night
I told you my father had told me that I
should be "realistic" about the whole psychology th___
I had been getting kind of discourged because
_____ see myself reaching that goal, but any___
___ made me realize that I shouldn't give up
___ dream.
     I read your poem, you are so sweet and
love you so much! It means alot to me to
know you love me just as much. As you kno___
___ have a hard time expressing myself to you and __
have to apologize for that because I know i__
frustrating for you. But ░░░░ love you uncon___
with all my heart. You make me a very happy p__
__ah I may be seventeen, and I dont, lots g__
___ ___ nor do I know which direction I

The disappointment I had with myself prevented me from enjoying high school. I even refused to walk across the stage for graduation. I had my mind set on who I wanted to be and what I wanted to accomplish. Being a mom at seventeen, wasn't it.

I often wondered what my life would have been like if I hadn't gotten pregnant. My friends were talking about college applications, prom plans, and college tours. I, on the other hand, was trying to manage my low progesterone levels to maintain a healthy pregnancy. It was a lonely feeling watching everyone else move forward with their lives while mine stood still. My future, once so clear, suddenly felt blurry and out of reach.

Even though I tried to stay strong on the outside, the judgment from classmates, teachers, and even family members chipped away at my confidence. Every glance felt like an accusation, every whisper like a condemnation. I didn't need them to tell me I'd made a mistake, I was already my own harshest critic. But no matter how much I berated myself, the fact remained: I was going to be a mom, and that realization terrified me.

Statistics often paint a bleak picture, suggesting that less than 50% of teen mothers graduate from high school, and only 2% earn a college degree by the age of thirty. I knew the odds were stacked against me, but my mom's unwavering belief in education was a lifeline. She kept reminding me that this wasn't the end of my dreams, just a detour. My dad, always practical, said, "Get a skill, something you can rely on to take care of yourself and your child." At the time, it felt like they were speaking two different languages, one of hope and the other of harsh reality.

I feel like shame is compounding. It builds on itself; layer on top of layer, like a heavy weight that becomes more difficult to carry with every misstep or perceived failure. Every single infraction, every mistake, every harsh word directed toward you, or moment of rejection by anyone adds to the bucket of self-deprecation, making the sense of unworthiness fundamentally deeper. It can seem as though shame holds you in a loop, where you can become trapped in a cycle, where every new wound serves as a reminder of past pain. It thrives in silence and grows in the shadows, feeding off the belief that you are not enough.

This compounding shame doesn't just weigh down your spirit, it obscures your vision. It blocks the line of sight along the path to empowerment, narrowing your world until all you can see are your faults. It distorts your sense of self, making it nearly impossible to recognize your worth, your strengths, or the potential within you.

When you're buried under the weight of shame, the idea of empowerment feels distant, almost impossible to reach. You're so focused on the parts of yourself that you deem unworthy or broken that you lose sight of the fact that you are capable of healing and growth.

Shame is insidious because it convinces you that the problem is you, not your circumstances or your experiences. It tells you that you are flawed at your core, and that belief becomes self-reinforcing. Every challenge, every obstacle, every moment of self-doubt just adds more fuel to the fire, convincing you that empowerment is for other people, not for you. It becomes harder to see the possibilities of what you can be when you're constantly reminded of who you think you are not.

But shame is a lie. It is not the truth of who you are. The longer you allow it to compound, the harder it is to break free, but that doesn't mean freedom isn't possible. Empowerment begins when you acknowledge shame for what it is,a barrier to your potential, a fog that clouds your vision. The first step toward breaking its hold is understanding that you are not defined by your worst moments, nor are you limited by your past.

As long as you allow shame to weigh you down, it will continue to hold you back. But if you begin to release the layers of that shame, piece by piece, infraction by infraction, you will make room for self-compassion, forgiveness, and grace. With each release, you clear the path a little more, and the line of sight to empowerment becomes less obstruct- ed. It is not easy, but it is possible. The moment you decide to confront your shame is the moment you take the first step toward reclaiming your power.

In time, the burden of shame can be replaced with the realization that you are worthy, that your mistakes do not define you, and that the path to empowerment has always been yours to walk.

I didn't entirely give up on pursuing my dream of being a psychologist at that time. Still, I knew that I needed that skill my father was advising me to get so that I could take care of my son. I took an eight-week class to become a certified nursing assistant. I knew I didn't want to be a nurse, but this gave me an opportunity to find a job quickly. My son's grandmother had a good friend who taught the class. To show support, my mom also took the class with me.

While having a nursing assistant certificate was great, the reality of finding a job and figuring out childcare was complex. Most of the time, my son, my boyfriend, and I laid around and enjoyed being with each other. He finally came back to Illinois to be with us, and that was enough for me. We ate take-out and watched T.V. That was short-lived, though. His mother wasn't going to allow him to live with her, and I wasn't allowed to sleep over. He ended up finding a studio apartment. My son and I were there all the time. My parents had the same rule his mom did. I wasn't allowed to sleep at his place.

My parents made it very clear that they weren't raising another kid. My little brother was five at the time, and my sister was seven. They had to raise their children and would not allow me to disrupt the rules of their home. Going rogue and having a child didn't change the rigid structure that my stepdad had established. I did my best to adhere to their rules, but with no car, I still depended on my boyfriend to get me back and forth home.

I spent New Year's Eve with my little family. When it was time for me to get back home, my boyfriend decided that he wasn't getting up to take me back that night. He let me know that he'd take me back in the morning. A part of me was happy about it. Not that I wanted to rebel against my parents, but I never wanted to stop playing house with my little family. My mom warned me that if I stayed out all night, I would not be able to come back. Sure enough, when my boyfriend took me back to my parent's home the next morning, I was met outside with my mom and a laundry basket filled with my belongings. I was asked to leave.

I wasn't in any way offended that my parents put me out initially. I wanted to be a family with my son and my boyfriend, anyway. I thought he wanted the same. In the letters he wrote to me, he told me about his dreams of being a family with me. He promised me a life full of joy and love. This picture was painted with the brush strokes of my deep yearning to have love, to have a family. What I wasn't aware of, was the pressure and stress he was feeling. I would hear him on the phone complaining about the responsibility of taking care of me and my son. He needed my financial support. His frustration grew and turned into him acting out violently.

I lived with him a couple months before the first time he was violent toward me. The incident happened one night, seemingly out of the blue. I had spilled a glass of coke on the carpet. He exploded and put his hands around my neck as he pushed me into the walk-in closet, past his clothes, slamming me against the wall. I was in shock. I grew up seeing fighting and violence between the people I loved, but I couldn't believe that it was happening to me.

Afterward, he apologized. He explained to me how his parents were abusive toward him. It would be the first of many times I heard about how his father broke his jaw. Time and time again, I'd hear about the day his mother broke his arm with a broom. This night was the first of many I'd heard about the day his stepdad beat him for not wearing a coat outside. This was the first of many nights my heart ached so intensely that I felt like it actually would break within the cavities of my chest. He hurt me, but I wanted him to comfort me from the pain he inflicted. How was it that the person who had caused me such grief seemed like the only remedy for the pain?

The stories from his broken childhood made me believe he had potential to be a great man, so I was convinced he was just not loved properly. I went along with him, and I blamed his parents for his angry outbursts. I thought he just had a bad break in life, and as soon as things got better for us, there would be no reason for him to be so angry ever again. I didn't want to be a burden. I wanted to contribute, so I knew I had to get a job.

The cycle: The calm, peaceful, and what can even seem like joyful times are what you live for. They're the moments that give you hope, a glimpse of what life could be like if things were different. You savor those times because they feel like a reward, a brief escape from the chaos. In those moments, you tell yourself that maybe things are finally getting better, maybe the worst is behind you. But even as you enjoy the peace, there's a part of you that's always waiting. Waiting for the other shoe to drop. You've learned, through experience, that it's only a matter of time.

You start walking on eggshells, trying to prolong the peace, to do everything right, to avoid anything that might set them off. Every word and every action is measured. You become hyper-aware of their mood, the change in their tone of voice, their body language when they interact with you. Your people pleasing is fully activated. You read every little sign, hoping to anticipate the moment when things shift. The tension is always there, simmering just beneath the surface. You can feel it even if you can't always name it. It's there, lurking in the quiet moments, casting a shadow over the joy you're trying so very hard to hold onto as you feel tensions rising.

Then, it happens. Sometimes, it's a slow build, a subtle change in their demeanor. Other times, it's a sudden snap over something small, something you didn't even realize would be a trigger. But it's never really about the thing that sets them off. All of this is actually about control, power, and the constant need to remind you that peace is conditional and that joy comes with a price.

The emotional distance grows, and with it, the fear. You brace yourself, knowing what's coming but feeling powerless to stop it.

The eruption is inevitable, like a storm you've seen gathering in the distance. And when it hits, it's devastating. You tell yourself that maybe this time will be different, that maybe the outburst will stop at yelling, at harsh words that sting but don't leave visible scars. But deep down, you know better. The blow lands and the cycle repeats. The shock, the pain, the humiliation,it all comes rushing back, even though part of you knew it was coming. What's left is the aftermath of the physical pain, and the emotional wreckage.

The next morning, you stand in front of the mirror, layering on makeup, it doesn't matter how much you apply; you can still feel the bruise underneath. It's not just the swelling of your eye or the discoloration of your skin that you're trying to hide. It's the shame, the fear, the self-blaming. You hope no one notices. You hope they don't ask questions because what could you possibly say? You've become skilled at hiding the signs, not just from others but from yourself. You convince yourself that this is just how it is, that the peace you crave will return eventually if you can just make it through this storm.

And so, the cycle continues. Clinging to the good times, the moments of calm, you find yourself dreading the next eruption. You have learned to navigate the emotional landmines, trying to do whatever it takes to avoid setting them off, even though deep down, you know that it's really not in your control. The peace, the joy, the calm,they're fleeting, always overshadowed by the looming threat of what's to come.

Night Shift

My first job as a nursing assistant was at a group home for severely developmentally disabled adults. It was vastly different from the job I had at the grocery store or Old Navy when I was a 16 year old. The population we served at the group home had disabilities that prevented them from being able to walk, talk, feed themselves, or even use the bathroom. These clients were chronologically fully grown adults but had the mental capacity of a five-month-old. Much like the five-month-old I had at home, they depended entirely on someone for care. As I was learning to care for my infant, I was exercising those caretaking skills at work as well.

I couldn't afford the cost of a daycare facility for my son, not even with the subsidized program from the government. I had to find a home daycare, which was much more affordable than the facilities. Finding someone I trusted with my baby wasn't easy, but I didn't have a choice. I found a seemingly nice lady close to my job. She had a big, beautiful home and took care of other children. She didn't speak the best English but took care of my son for about a week.

One morning, I dropped him off. The caregiver opened the door disheveled, with a black eye that looked like whatever caused it was pretty painful. I asked what happened and she said she went dancing and caught an elbow to the face. I had to pry my son off my hip because he didn't want to go with her.

That afternoon, I went to pick my son up from the babysitter. The small-framed woman opened the door with him in her arms. He looked like he had been crying all day, with dried tears on his cheeks and snot crusted on his nose. My heart ached. As she handed me my son, "I can't keep him anymore. I'm sorry. He won't stop crying," she said with her thick Polish accent. Between the man I had never seen before in the background and the woman's bruised and swollen eye, I gathered that the situation may have been unsafe and gladly took my son never to return.

The responsibility of finding childcare so that I could work, seemed to rest on my shoulders alone. I took some time off work to figure out what I would do about child-care. Luckily, I was able to find someone who became a godsend. The new caregiver loved my son as if he were her own. My son loved being there, and I knew he was safe. Rachel became a trusted friend during a difficult time while I was trying to figure out how to be a young, working mom.

My boyfriend, my son, and I lived in a studio apartment, trying to make being a family work. I'd often find my boyfriend watching old videos of himself playing high school basketball. I think he often fantasized about what life would have been like if he had focused on playing ball throughout college. I don't think he had ambitions to play in the NBA, but for him, basketball was the one thing that made him feel special. In a large way, I believe he felt like I had taken that away from him. At that time, I was there with him in his studio apartment to remind him of his choices, and I paid for that.

The slightest infraction turned into something awful. My boyfriend found himself doing well at his job, and we decided to get a bigger place. We secured a two-bedroom apartment, and we were excited to move. The last thing we needed to do was to switch over the cable. He asked me to do that just in time for him to be able to watch a basketball game that night. I forgot and he was furious. I don't know why I forgot, but it didn't happen when he wanted it to happen. He called me names, and I called him names. Then, he spit in my face.

There was a time when I was a child visiting my aunt Michelle. Back then, she was married to her husband, uncle Jim. I would never forget how extremely abusive he was toward her. I was really young, so I didn't understand what was going on, but I remember that the violence struck this intense amount of fear in me. My cousin and I were in the car one day, and uncle Jim was yelling at aunt Michelle. I remember papers suddenly flying everywhere in the street, and then he spit in her face. I remember feeling disgusted and worried, wondering what would happen next. I vowed that I wouldn't let someone do that to me and get away with it. There's something so very degrading about someone spitting on you. The amount of disregard someone has to have for another, is inhumane.

After he spat in my face, he picked up our son and headed out the back patio door. At that moment, the fact that he so casually walked away infuriated me. I reacted, and as that man began to walk out the door, I punched him. With every ounce of strength I had, I hit him in the back of the head and punched him in the back. Why did I do that? He turned around, sat our son down, and clocked me right in the face. He didn't stop hitting me. Over and over again, I felt his rage. I had never been in a fight before, so being punched in the face was devastating.

Of course, later that evening, I got his version of how I lost it and was acting crazy. I got the sob story of how he blacked out and didn't know what he was doing. He had a way of making me feel like it was my fault, followed up by a come-to-Jesus moment that encompassed some "aha actualization" that was going to prompt a drastic change in our relationship. In his remorseful stage he told me he stopped because I passed out for a moment.

The condo we were going to move into was foreclosed with all of the things we had just moved over to the place. The owner gave us no warning about the financial standing of the condo we were about to rent. Sean had to call a locksmith to get our belongings out. As I stood there with a black eye, the locksmith had a disturbing look on his face. He tried to look away, but we both felt his discomfort. Sean sent me away to grab something from the studio apartment.

I left to go but wanted to ask a question, so I turned around. Before I knocked on the door, I heard him talking to the locksmith. "You know, sometimes you have to do what you have to do so they'll listen, you know." He was justifying why he beat my ass, as if, man to man, this stranger would side with him.It wasn't long before I took my son and left a letter letting Sean know I was leaving. I didn't give any warning; I just left.

Eventually, I somewhat made amends with my parents, and my mom helped me find an apartment. My mom wanted to keep the peace in her home. At that point, I knew that going back to my parent's home wasn't an option. My step dad established that they weren't going to have a revolving door. I had burned the bridge that led back to my parent's house. The same angst my mom had about keeping things peaceful in her home, was something I carried as well. From childhood, I adopted the idea that my behavior impacted their marriage. It felt like my responsibility to make sure I wasn't a problem for my stepdad. It was never something anyone told me directly, but in some ways, the weight of trying not to be an issue in their marriage, created a fragmented relationship between us.

My mom helped me find my way to self-sufficiency by living on my own as much as possible. I was nineteen with no credit—so, she cosigned at a place right around the corner from where they lived. She agreed to give me $200 a month to help with rent. I was proud to have my own place, but I ended up working sixteen-hour shifts most days to make ends meet. My little one-bedroom apartment had no furniture, and me and my son, Metri, slept on a mattress on the floor. I worked the night shift at the group home and the day shift when my son was at daycare. Still, it wasn't even enough for me to maintain holding down a place of my own. I gave up on my apartment and moved back in with my son's father.

I was cordial with my son's father, and we co-parented when I lived in my own place. We were both moving on, but then, we slipped up. That slip-up got me pregnant again. The first thing I thought about was getting an abortion. I made two appointments: one for the OB/GYN and one for the abortion clinic.

I had an abortion before—it was a terrifying experience. I woke up out of anesthesia and had a full anxiety attack. In my subconscious, I thought that I died. I wasn't sure I could go through it again. Not to mention, my religious upbringing was rooted in the belief that an abortion was incredibly wrong. So, I prayed. On my way to the clinic I had this unsettling feeling that this was not the right decision. I felt like I should have the child. Something, I believe God, told me that it would be a boy. At that moment, I knew his name would be Isaiah. Little did I know, he'd be my saving grace.

It is the small voice that guides you. The one that whispers when everything else is loud; steady even when chaos is all around you. We pray for signs, for something major and unmistakable, but God's direction is often subtle, almost unnoticeable. It's not always the dramatic revelation we expect; it's the quiet subtle nudge, the soft push in the right direction, the feeling that rests in your heart long after the noise fades. It's in these moments of stillness that you come to understand that divine guidance doesn't always shout,it waits for you to listen.

To hear that voice, you have to be still and pay attention. You have to tune out the loudness of the world, the distractions, the doubts, and all the things that pull you away from your center. Fear, shame, guilt, and pain,they scream for your attention, creating so much noise that it drowns out the very guidance you seek. They cloud your judgment, drown out your thoughts, and make it difficult to trust the path that's unfolding before you. These emotions can feel all-consuming, but they are not the truth of who you are. They are barriers that block the connection to the divine voice within you.

When you allow yourself to silence the noise, even for just a moment, you open up space to feel that subtle yet profound guidance. It may not be the answer you expected or wanted, but it will always be what you need. It may come in the form of an idea that reveals itself in your mind, a feeling of peace in your heart, or even an unexpected opportunity that presents itself at the right time. These moments feel like divine clarity. They can be so gentle that if you're not paying attention, you might miss them.

It's in those still, reserved spaces that you learn to trust. Trust that you are being led; trust that even in the absence of clear signs, you are being guided. Trust that God is present, not always in the loud, miraculous moments, but in the small, everyday ones. Trust that the answers you are looking for are already within you, waiting for the noise to subside so they can be heard.

God's direction is not always about the destinationt'; it's about each step along the journey. And sometimes, that step is simply to be still, to listen, and to trust that the voice you hear, no matter how faint, is leading you toward something greater than you can imagine.

Isaiah

I felt a similar sense of shame being pregnant again, though not as intensely as when I was seventeen. Still, I had no desire to have another child with Sean at that time. I kept working the night shift at the group home and sometimes stayed over to work during the day. But as my pregnancy progressed, it became harder to keep up with the heavy lifting in addition to being on my feet for sixteen-hour shifts.

Without the extra income, I could no longer afford daycare, so my son had to stop going to Racheal. I'd come home from work at 7 o'clock in the morning, get him breakfast, and spend some time with him before attempting to nap while he watched TV. I usually only slept a few hours once his father came home, just before I had to leave for my next shift.

Living with Sean was difficult, especially knowing he didn't honestly want to be in a relationship with me. Despite his apparent disinterest, he still expected me to act like a partner. I knew he was seeing another woman. She'd drive by our apartment wearing big sunglasses and a hat as if that would keep me from noticing. It hurt, not because I wanted to be with him, but because I longed for the family life I imagined we could have had. I desperately wanted to create the type of family I desired as a child—more than I actually wanted him. The dream of being a family and raising my children with their father, was something I clung to more than anything else. It was an idea that had taken root in my heart because I didn't have that as a child. I became bound to this idea of what an ideal family looked like. The vow I made to myself caused me more pain because my life did not replicate what I hoped my future would be.

Even though I was eventually raised in a two-parent household, the attention in our home shifted to my mom and stepdad raising my younger sister and brother. I felt the sense of belonging drift away. It was my mom, her husband, and their two children. As a teen, I felt disconnected despite the fact that I was well taken care of as a child. My stepdad had taught me so much about life. He showed me what hard work looked like. He taught me everything from how to wash dishes properly to changing a tire. In those days, I didn't fully appreciate how much he was teaching me, but I was always grateful for the time we spent together. He was tough on me at times, as men born in the 1950s often were with their children. When I was 16 years old and we moved to our first home, he insisted I get a job. He dropped me off on the busiest street in the neighborhood that was lined with chain stores and restaurants. He told me to apply at each one. While he cringes when I bring it up now, that experience taught me determination.

When my biological father stopped coming around, my mom and stepdad proposed the idea of my stepdad adopting me. "Will I have to change my last name? I like my last name," I said, politely declining. I didn't fully understand the significance of their offer at the time; I just liked being a "Jones." I also still felt a sense of loyalty to my father, and adopting my stepdad's name felt like giving up on him.

There was still this dilema of how to fuse me into the blended family. With the arrival of my younger sister, we came up with a name for my stepdad that wasn't his first or last name, "papa." That worked for me. He was someone I admired deeply, and we had a great relationship. It worked for our family—until my sister started talking. She didn't call him, "daddy," and that became an issue. So, they decided I should stop calling him, "papa" too. I didn't know what to call him , so I called him nothing for a while. I eventually started calling him, "dad," but it felt like a betrayal at first, even though I had accepted him as my father figure.

I didn't want my own children to experience that same confusion, split loyalties or feelings of not belonging. I vowed not to raise my kids in a divided family. So, I held on to the hope that their father would step up, especially when I found out I was pregnant with his second son. But he didn't, and eventually, I stopped caring. It wasn't him I wanted, it was the idea of who I wished he could be. I realized I never truly knew him. I had created an image of who I needed him to be in order to fill the void left by my own father's absence. At the time I accepted there would never be a real relationship with him. I was exhausted; I just wanted to find a place for my two boys and me to live. In my mind, I was done having children.

As a teenager, I had once wanted four kids, like my aunt Michelle. But after multiple unexpected pregnancies, I decided that was enough. However, my OB/GYN disagreed.

At my eight-month checkup, I told the nurse practitioner that I wanted to get my tubes tied. She looked at me and said, "You're too young to make that decision. What if you lose both of your children in a car accident?" I was stunned. I was twenty years old, struggling to survive and take care of my child, with another on the way, stuck in an abusive relationship I was trying to escape. I knew I couldn't handle more children, yet there she was, trying to convince me otherwise. "You'll want to have more children if something happens," she continued, "Besides, you're only twenty."

I knew exactly how old I was, and I knew what I wanted for my life and my body. I didn't need anyone making that decision for me or speaking death over my children. It was upsetting, I knew my limits, and I knew that to build a better future, I had to take control of my life, starting with my body.

April Showers

I always felt guilty coming home from the night shift, utterly exhausted and barely able to interact with Demetrius. Working the night shift was grueling, not just because of the hours, but because it took a toll on my body and mind. Most mornings, I would sit next to him on the couch, put on his favorite cartoon, and drift in and out of sleep. I wanted to do more and be more present, but my body felt like it was constantly running empty. There were moments when he would look up at me, his eyes full of curiosity and joy, and I'd feel a huge sense of guilt for not being able to engage more.

When the weather warmed up, I tried to push past the exhaustion. I made an effort to take Metri out, sometimes to the nearby petting zoo or for ice cream while running errands. He was my sweet baby boy, full of energy and joy—always making the best of any situation. He had a way of lighting up any room, his laughter so contagious that it could momentarily lift the weight I carried. I clung to those moments as a reminder that, despite the struggles, I was still doing my best for him.

By the time Demetrius was two and a half, I was in my third trimester with Isaiah. I remember the excitement in his eyes as he helped me put away the baby clothes. He assisted in folding tiny onesies and carefully stacking diapers. My two-year-old didn't fully understand what was coming but seemed to sense the change. He knew there was a baby on the way, and he was going to be a big brother. Even though I was exhausted from work and pregnancy, I cherished the thought of them growing up together, side by side. I imagined them playing, sharing toys, and getting into mischief. Sadly, they never got the chance to meet.

It was April 2, 2005. As always, I had just finished my shift and hurried home to say good morning to my little boy. My body ached from the long night, but seeing Demetrius always made the exhaustion worth it. That day, I had last-minute errands to run in preparation for the new baby. I had asked their father to watch Demetrius, but he couldn't stand being home. Without any warning, he left to go to work, even though it was his day off. It was just another example of how unreliable he had become.So, I decided to take Metri with me. We lived in Aurora, a western suburb of Chicago. It wasn't the best area, but finding affordable housing was a struggle. I relied on government programs like WIC to meet our basic needs, and I tried to make do with what we had. That day, I had an appointment downtown by the Fox River. Metri was so excited to be outside, bouncing with energy, his little hand gripping mine tightly. As we crossed a bridge, he stopped and pointed at the water below, his face lighting up with wonder. I paused with him, letting him soak in the moment. Those small, simple moments were everything to me.

Later, we stopped by a friend's house,my last errand before what I imagined would be hibernation as I waited for Isaiah's arrival. I was beyond tired and grateful to finally sit down. Metri, on the other hand, was restless and wanted to play outside with the other kids. I didn't feel comfortable letting him go too far, but I also felt guilty for not giving him the freedom to play like other kids. So, I let him stay where I could see him, thinking that would be safe enough.

One moment, he was in my sight, the next moment, he wasn't. It all happened so fast,one second of distraction, and my whole world changed. We scrambled to find him, calling his name and running in all directions. Deep down, I had this sinking feeling that something terrible had happened, but I kept praying that he was okay. I stood on the sidewalk, frozen, as my friend came up the small hill. She was holding his limp body across her arms; lifeless. My heart stopped.

She gently placed him on the sidewalk, and I froze. I knew I had to do something, but at that moment, I forgot everything. I forgot how to give CPR, how to move, how to breathe. My friend took over, performing chest compressions, and water came out of his mouth, but it wasn't like in the movies,there was no miraculous gasp for air, no sudden return to life. He just laid there, still.

The ambulance arrived, and I rode separately, my heart in my throat as they continued CPR on the way to the hospital. The paramedic tried to reassure me, telling me they'd seen cases like this before where the child survived. I clung to that hope, not ready to accept the possibility that my baby was gone. It all felt so surreal as if I were living in a nightmare that I couldn't wake up from.

At the hospital, Sean arrived angry and confused. His mother came, my mother came, and we all waited in silence, hoping for a miracle. But when the doctors came out with tears in their eyes, I knew. I knew before they even said the words. My legs gave out beneath me, and I collapsed to the floor. How could this be real? How could this be happening?

The rest of the day was a blur of faces, voices, and tears. At some point, the nurses suggested I hold him one last time. I cradled his tiny body in my arms, staring at his perfect little hands, devastated by how quickly life can be taken away. I placed him on my swollen belly, feeling his weight press down on the life still growing inside of me. Isaiah kicked as I held his brother, and the contrast of life and death in that moment was too much to bear. I wanted to freeze time, to stay in that moment forever, but the contractions were coming harder now.

Losing Demetrius at two years old shattered me in ways I couldn't have imagined. The pain was suffocating, like an anchor pulling me down into darkness. I was only 20 years old, still learning how to navigate life, and suddenly, I was hit with this unimaginable loss. It felt like the world had stopped turning. Every step forward felt like an act of betrayal. How could I keep going without my son?

The guilt weighed heavily on my shoulders, wrapping itself around every memory I had of him. Every decision I made that day, every moment where I thought he'd be okay,it all replayed in my mind, taunting me. I kept thinking "what if I hadn't taken him out that day? What if I had watched him more closely? What if…?" The questions were endless, and the answers were unbearable. It was like I was responsible for not only losing my child but for destroying the life that could have been his.

There's a deep shame that comes with losing a child, even though it wasn't my fault. I felt like I had failed him. How could I have let something like this happen? I was his mother—I was supposed to protect him from the world, but in the blink of an eye, he was gone. People tried to comfort me, but their words fell flat. I felt undeserving of their sympathy because I believed I should have been able to stop it.

Then there was the pain. The kind that never really goes away. It lives inside you, finding new ways to remind you of the loss at the most unexpected moments. Every time I saw a child around Demetrius's age, my heart would ache. Every birthday that passed without him felt like a wound reopening. It wasn't just emotional pain, it was physical. My chest hurt, my body was heavy, and my mind was constantly exhausted, trying to make sense of the senseless.

Prior to the accident, my only experience with death was losing my grandfather a few months before. He was older and struggled with multiple health conditions. We saw him weaken over the years—anticipating that his time would come. I never experienced tragic loss in a way that Metri's death hit.

Being only twenty years old made it even harder. I was barely an adult, but here I was, thrust into a situation that no one should ever have to experience. I was expected to grieve, to heal, and to somehow keep moving forward when all I wanted was to go back in time and change everything. Yet, I had to snap right back into motherhood. My needs, as an individual, didn't matter; at least that's how I felt. Isaiah was ready to enter the world to a mother that was terrified to receive him. I had already lost one child, and I wasn't sure I could handle the responsibility of another. The thought of loving again, of opening myself up to the possibility of loss, was paralyzing. How could I do this when my heart was still shattered? I questioned my ability to parent again and at the same time, that was the only thing keeping me tethered to this earth.

Given my state of mind, I don't think I would have had the will to live.... Fifteen days after Demetrius died, on a Sunday, Isaiah was born.

Your brain doesn't fully develop until the age of twenty or so. The parts responsible for decision-making, emotional regulation, and impulse control are still forming well into early adulthood. So, when trauma occurs in those critical developmental years, it has a profound impact on how you perceive the world and how you navigate through it. Trauma doesn't just leave emotional scars; it rewires your brain, altering your ability to process experiences, regulate your behavior, and make decisions. You start to see the world through the lens of what happened to you, not what could be, and it colors every aspect of your life.

When trauma sets in, it's not just a memory, it becomes a blueprint. You adapt to your environment, consciously or unconsciously, based on those traumatic events, and that adaptation becomes the foundation for how you approach life's challenges. It's a survival mechanism, a way to protect yourself from further harm. But while these adaptations may help you survive in the moment, they often limit your ability to thrive long term. You end up reacting to situations based on the trauma you've experienced rather than responding with clarity and intention. You learn to expect the worst, anticipate danger, and brace for impact even when it's not there.

This kind of adaptation can make it difficult to trust others, to trust yourself, or to feel safe even in calm moments. You might find yourself avoiding situations that remind you of past pain, shutting down emotionally, or becoming hyper-vigilant. What was once a defense mechanism, suddenly becomes a way of life, shaping your worldview and your approach to challenges. Trauma convinces you that your past experiences are the ultimate truth. You adapt by building walls around yourself and staying in survival mode long after the threat has passed.

But here's the thing, while trauma may shape your initial responses to life, it doesn't have to define them forever. The brain is capable of change. With healing, intentional work, and support, you can rewire those pathways. You can learn new ways to approach life's challenges,to self-regulate, and to create a worldview based on empowerment rather than fear. Trauma may have impacted how you once saw the world, but it doesn't have to dedicate how you see it tomorrow.

Fight Flight Freeze

As a kid, if we were at Granny's house when a storm came, we'd cut off the TV, lights, and anything electrical. We'd just sit in the dark. Me and my cousins would sometimes take refuge under the large oak dining room table. We'd sit in the dark and sing hymns. No matter if it was just heavy rain or an actual tornado warning, Granny would always remind us that God was speaking. We were taught to believe that if something bad was happening, God was smiting someone for their sins.

I felt like the loss of my son was my fault in every regard, including retribution for my sins. I decided that I needed to be the perfect Christian in order to detour God from further punishment in my life. I spent the next nine years trying to be the perfect saint, wife, and mother. I studied the Bible like I was in seminary. We attended church a couple times a week. We attempted to do everything perfect in an effort to atone for our sins. That included getting married.

Let me tell you the worst way to heal from a loss:

Step 1: Get married.

Two months after we lost our son and had the second, we got married. We made a major life decision in the middle of grieving, and to be fair, we were grieving poorly. Sean became my husband. Mind you, we weren't even together when the tragedy struck. He expressed that he didn't want to have another child with me.

We ended up being bound together because of the traumatic experience. He and I were the only two who understood the pain we were going through. We thugged it out, together, with no coping skills at hand to pull from. He grieved his way, and I didn't grieve at all. We poured all of our attention and energy into being parents for Isaiah.

At my son's repass, before our actual courthouse wedding, people kept coming up to me smiling. "Sean told me you got married!" First, my father asked as he gave us wedding gifts he managed to put together just before the funeral. I was in complete shock from having to bury my son. I couldn't gather what was actually going on. Then, the pastor who gave the eulogy came up to congratulate us. He had the biggest smile and a sense of pride. I was silent. I was in disbelief that he was telling everyone we got married. The repass was held at Sean's mother's house. I was completely overwhelmed by the attention. My mother found me, and with complete confusion, she asked about this alleged secret marriage. I told her that Sean was telling everyone that we got married. To this day, I am not sure why he did that. He was always concerned about how people perceived him.

I found my way upstairs to the room we were staying in at his mother's house during the repass. I couldn't return back to the apartment and see Metri's toys and clothes around. We stayed at his mother's home until we found a new place.

I needed a break from the chaos and noise of the people that gathered at the repass. I couldn't take the glares of pity. In front of everyone, Sean acted like a devoted "husband," but behind closed doors, he was intentional about making sure I carried the guilt for the loss of our son.

Sean's friend, and former high school basketball coach, gifted us with a trip to Florida for our "honeymoon." We actually had to get married before we took the trip. A couple months later, we went to the courthouse and said our nuptials. The judge held Isaiah as we exchanged vows and rings.

I was excited about being a wife. I had no comprehensive knowledge of what it meant to be a good wife. I was just happy to have the title. It was a fresh start for me. I felt like it was a fresh start for our relationship. I went into it naive, thinking that being married was actually the reset I desired. In reality, it was the continuation of something awful built on a dysfunctional foundation.

I went back to work eventually. In the span of my maternity leave, I lost a child, had a child, and got married. I was happy to be back around people and doing things to stay busy. I tried to feel normal again. I continued to work at the group home and enjoyed the sense of familiarity and routine. My co-workers embraced me and tried to be supportive. I needed that more than I realized. The initial empathetic responses to my circumstance had forced me to put on this mask to show everyone I was okay, and that they didn't have to act all sad around me. Truth was, I was hurting badly inside, but I did my best not to let it show.

I strongly desired to connect with someone who could understand the type of pain and loss I was experiencing. My new husband often sat and watched a DVD with the slideshow of all the pictures we rounded together for the funeral. I couldn't even bring myself to look at pictures. I wanted an example of how to get through this that I could relate to. I met with one psychologist who shared his experience with his wife having a miscarriage. While very painful, it wasn't like my loss. I needed to see someone who had shared the experience of having the laughter of your child snatched away from you in an instant. Metri didn't talk much, but he would always call for me like Stewie from Family Guy, "Mom, mommy, mommy, mommy." It haunted me not to hear that.

Who could I explain that to? Who would understand?

I worked with a couple nurses who had tragedy touch their lives. One nurse lost her husband to suicide. You could see the deep hurt and anger when Sally talked about him. When the anniversary of his death came around, I saw her crying in the kitchen, away from everyone in an attempt to hide what she was feeling. She hated what he did. She struggled to make peace with the tragedy that struck her family. She was always short-tempered and often lashed out at her staff.

When I came back to work, there was a new nurse who had started in the group home, Nancy. She had heard about my tragedy and offered a sentiment of condolences for my loss. She was someone you could tell had been through a difficult time in life. A little rough around the edges. We hung back one day after getting the clients up and ready for the day. The three of us talked about how our losses impacted our lives. The new nurse talked about how she lost her daughter to SIDS (Sudden Infant Death Syndrome). With a newborn at home, I was terrified as she explained that she just woke up and her child was dead. She explained how she was angry with God, and she just didn't understand why that had happened to her.

Talking to these women didn't give me much hope on how to cope with this kind of loss. It did, however, make me realize how I didn't want to approach my grief. I still wasn't quite sure how to navigate through life with this immense pain, but I did know that I wanted to be happy. I wanted to laugh again. I wanted to actually have a desire to be intimate with my husband, but I didn't know how to get there. I completely lost touch with who I was and just wore a mask, hoping no one would see my pain. I wanted to bury it so far that I couldn't feel it. The problem was that I buried myself.

I tried to hold on to pieces of my old life, but the reality was that I was on a different path. Sean lost his job at the nursing home when we lost our son. It seemed cruel to let him go at such a time, but the owner of the facility thought that he may struggle to fulfill his duties as a mental health professional after that experience. He decided to go back to school full-time while I worked. He stayed home with Isaiah during the day and went to school in the evening. I tried taking a couple classes myself but ultimately spent my time helping him get through school. I was so proud of his accomplishment that I didn't recognize the effort I put in to help him get there.

All of my friends went off to college while I was busy being a wife and mom, but I kept in touch with my best friend. Tamia was by my side through it all. When everyone else kind of went on with their lives while I was pregnant in high school, she tried to stay connected. Her family even threw me a baby shower when we were in high school. I needed some connection to who I used to be, while wearing a mask for the world to see. When she came home from school, I made sure we spent time together. Sean never really cared for her. I'm not really sure why, other than it seemed like any relationship I had outside of him was somewhat of a threat. Tamia and her boyfriend were home from school around the holidays for break and she wanted me to meet him. They came by the apartment while Sean was at school. I told him I was going to meet them at the club house. The apartment complex had this beautiful club house with a racketball court, pool table, and gym. I figured I could respect Sean's wishes not to have people over when he wasn't home but also see my best friend.

It was late by the time she was able to come around with her new boyfriend. It was Isaiah's bedtime, and I could not go to the clubhouse, so I invited them over. As we sat on the couch, Sean called. I answered. "You better not have nobody in my house!" He yelled through the phone. I figured he was in class, and by the time he got out of class, they'd be gone. Tamia's boyfriend picked up on the tension and suggested that they leave. As they were putting on their shoes to leave, Sean swooped in, hitting her boyfriend with the door, making sure we all felt his presence.

"What did I tell you?" Widening his eyes and tightening his lips. I knew what was coming, but I asked calmly, "Can you let me say bye and let them leave?" I said my goodbyes and closed the door. He began ranting, and before I knew it, I was being dragged by my braids from the living room to the bedroom. Later, Tamia told me they had sat in the parking lot for a minute before pulling off.

I was on the bed trying to protect myself while he was standing over me, throwing punches. He paused as his legs stood on each side of me. I saw the opening as an opportunity to get away. I attempted to kick him in the nuts. I figured that would debilitate him enough for me to fight back. I missed. I didn't think he could get angrier, but he went into rage mode. He punched harder and harder. A few landed on the left side of my face. I still have nerve damage in my face from that night.

The swelling went down enough for me to cover the bruising with makeup just in time for me to visit my family for Christmas. Sean told me I wouldn't be going to Christmas dinner if my eye was still swollen. I told Tamia about what happened. I expressed how happy I was that the swelling finally went down, minimizing the actual violence. I was more concerned about spending Christmas with my family. "Xavia, why would you want to keep that from your family?" Tamia never understood why I allowed myself to be treated that way. Why would I be more concerned about protecting his behavior than protecting my safety?

After each fight, a piece of me died until very little of the my essence was traceable. I eventually just did what he said to avoid confrontation.

This was the time in my life when I was just… frozen. In the book, The Body Keeps Score, by Van Der Kolk, Kolk talks about the autonomic nervous system, which is what activates the fight, flight or freeze response. This is how your body responds to traumatic events. There were times when fighting back was instinctual. But I wasn't dealing with someone who would back down, not even from a fight he knew he'd win. I tried to flee a few times but the weight of trying to make it on my own felt too heavy. Now, being completely broken from the death of my son, I didn't have as much left in me except doing whatever I needed to survive. I knew that if I had the slightest thought of leaving, he'd take my son. I was reminded, constantly, that I was responsible for what happened to Metri. That made it easy to supress the thoughts of leaving—I couldn't let him take my

Isaiah.

I lost touch with the friends I grew up with and just focused on being a good Christian wife and mom. Outside of my therapist, no one knew the extent of the fights. She supported me through my grieving process and tried to help me through the violence in my marriage. She always told me to leave a paper trail and to make sure I had an exit strategy if I had to leave abruptly.

I called the police. I never pressed charges though. He even spent a night in jail for ripping the door handle off my car when I was trying to get away. For a moment, I thought if I hit him with my car, he'd stop. Instead, I just filed a police report. I filed many police reports. The neighbors even called the police. I could only go as far as filing a report. I kept that all away from my family. The life we had in our home was very different from the one portrayed to everyone else.

By the time I was 23 years old, I was having my third son. I prayed for Joe. I had two miscarriages after Isaiah. I knew that no one would take the place of Metri, but I gave up on my own desires and played toward the pain of guilt, so I overcompensated with more children.

Why didn't you just leave? A question that many ask and, on the surface, may sound like a reasonable suggestion. The answer to that is extremely complex.

I was approaching my third trimester with Joe when I made an attempt to get away. Sean and I were lying in bed one night watching TV. I was texting my friend, who happened to be Sean's cousin's girlfriend, when he snatched my phone out of nowhere and began reading my messages. Ciera and I became good friends, and I confided in her a lot. He came across a message mentioning his name. "Give me my phone back!" I demanded. WHOP! I got a backhand to the face. I tasted the blood from my busted lip. Though very pregnant, I was thin and still limber. I kicked him. Somehow, my flexibility allowed my kick to land right in his face. His nose began bleeding, and so he was set off. He began choking me. I wrestled to get away from him and landed between the foot of the bed and the dresser. He straddled over my belly as he took a pillow placed over my face. Using all his strength, he pressed down. I couldn't breathe. He was suffocating me. I thought this was it; he was going to kill me. I panicked. I was kicking, screaming, and clawing at his arms as I fought for my life.

He released me, and I ran out of our apartment. It was late, and I didn't know where to go. I began having contractions, so I went to the emergency room and stayed the night. I had just stopped working because the doctor indicated that I had a high-risk pregnancy—I could no longer do the heavy lifting at the group home, so my job forced me to resign.

With no money and no place to go, I went back home, hoping the night apart would calm things down and cooler heads would prevail. "You know the police came last night looking for you," Sean told me. The neighbor upstairs called the police. "They saw my arms bleeding, and they wanted to lock you up, but I told them it was an accident," he went on, making sure I knew that he protected me from the police. There was a knock on the door. The neighbor did, in fact, call the police. Believing what he told me, without any evidence of him suffocating me with a pillow, I thought I was in trouble. "What happened last night?" The officer asked. I lied. In my naiveté, I went along with his story, hoping they wouldn't arrest me.

Shortly after that incident, I left to go visit my cousin. She lived about an hour away. We were making plans for Isaiah and me to come live with her. She was in nursing school while raising her daughter. She also volunteered to take care of her niece and nephew, so she had a house full. It wasn't long before I started wrestling with the idea of living so far from everything I knew. I told her I was concerned about my high-risk pregnancy and wanted to be closer to my doctors. While partially true, it was much less shallow than admitting I wanted to go back to my luxury apartment where my son could sleep in his racecar bed. I attempted to stay closer to where I established a life but I wasn't ready to go back to Sean. I went back to my parents' home and stayed for a while. I didn't tell my parents about the abuse. They were sympathetic after Metri's death. They figured we struggled to deal with the pain of our loss, so the more stringent boundaries that they once had were set aside for a short-term visit.

One evening, Sean asked to take me out while we were separated. We drove out to my son's grave site. A place I hated to go. It was night time, and I had no desire to be in a graveyard. He had flowers for me; this was a well thought out moment. He began his monologue, which he seemed to put a lot of thought into. He ended by saying he forgave me for what happened to Metri. "I'm leaving everything here in this graveyard. I'm going to bury it right here!" For a while, he did just that.

While the violence subsided for a while, other symptoms of our frail marriage began to surface. I didn't realize it at first, but he had relationships with some of the women he went to night school with and worked with. I picked up on something about a particular night school classmate because he talked about her so much.

There were many other women. He pretended that they were friends until, one day, he confessed that he had a sex addiction. He enrolled in a program and even had a sponsor to help him. On the weekends, we would attend support groups. He would go with the men; I went with the wives. It was the first time I heard someone talk about codependency.

Much like an AA meeting, they had to go through a 12-step process. You know, admit you're powerless. Step 8: Make a list of all persons you may have harmed. Step 9: Make direct amends to people when possible. All of that. One thing he had to do was confess all of his wrongdoings to me. The two of us sat in a room at the church where the sex-anon meeting was held. We were across the table from his sponsor and his sponsor's wife, when Sean pulled out a yellow legal pad with a list of names. One by one, he listed the women he had affairs with. His voice trembled as he detailed the confessions of his other life. I was disgusted, confused, and angry. I expected him to confirm one or two suspicions I had, but I was completely shocked. How did he even have time to have all these affairs? Another part of me died. No part of my life was real. I was living in the Matrix like Keanu Reeves' character, Neo. I was made to believe that my life was something that it wasn't. My husband was not the person he portrayed. He was only a fictitious character composed of my own ideas of a fantasy life I participated in.

Joe was six months old when I found out that I was pregnant with my daughter. I went to the doctor for back pain. Before prescribing muscle relaxers, the doctor asked, "Is there any chance you could be pregnant?" I chuckled and confidently said, "Absolutely not." "Well, let's just be sure," he asked me to take a pregnancy test. He came back to the room. "You are actually pregnant," he let me know. The room was filled with awkward silence as I sat in shock, jaw dropped. "I can't prescribe you this medication," he said, breaking the silence. Tied to my marriage even more, I wasn't at all excited about the news.

The impact of the affairs continued beyond Sean's, "coming to Jesus" moment. I remember getting an anonymous letter in the mail addressed to me, but the letter was a woman writing to Sean, reminiscing about their explicit love affair. The letter detailed how they met up during lunch hours at work. It gave specific details about their sexual interactions. He let me know that the woman was upset that he was now on this new path.

The part of me that needed to see the good in him (the

codependancy) blamed the addiction for his behavior. I believed that he was attempting to make a change. Convinced that if there was no violence and no cheating, he would be the perfect husband and father I needed him to be while also wrestling with the reality that he may never change. My codependency looked like excessive caretaking and a lack of ability to set boundaries. My ex-husband was my project. I needed to save him from himself, so I didn't have to face the possibility of becoming a single mother.

A woman from Sean's night school called me just before I gave birth to my daughter. She went into detail about how Sean was cheating on both of us basically. My unwanted sister-wife began to tell me about their four-year affair. Once Sean gave his confession, I became callous. She thought that I would have a different reaction, but I had no reaction. I just told her I was aware of everything she was telling me, even if I wasn't. "I love him like you love him," she told me as she was attempting to have this woman-to-woman conversation. "Well, that sounds dumb. I'm his wife," I responded. After I hung up, I called his mother and told her what happened. While I was talking to my mother-in-law, he burst through the door yelling and screaming,

"YOU DON'T KNOW WHAT JUST HAPPENED!"

I caught a glimpse out of the living room window to see that he had parked diagonally in the parking lot, and the driver's side door was left open. I know I was supposed to be concerned. I was supposed to panic as if some emergency needed my attention. He believed that his dramatic tactics would distract me from what was actually happening. "You don't understand what just happened!" He repeated. He desperately wanted me to think he was in distress. "I told her I was done. I'm about to have a daughter."

He was theatrically irate. Probably because he knew that she would be calling me. His mom came to the apartment after listening to him go crazy over the phone. He continued to put on the show even when she arrived. Sean was inconsolable, and I'm not sure why. He had escalated to the point his mother called the police after he picked her up to try to put her out of the apartment. The show continued. Even the police presence didn't sway him to calm down. We lived in a two-bedroom apartment with a small, beautifully decorated living room. In the middle of the living room, we had an iron and stone coffee table. It was a part of our first set of furniture we didn't have handed down. For some reason, that table became the recipient of Sean's frustration. When the Hulk was ranting and raving, he picked up the table and slammed it to the floor, breaking it to pieces. The police did nothing. I took my boys, and I left with my mother-in-law. I was about nine months pregnant at the time.

I was aware that if I stopped having children I would be in a better position to gain independence. I told my doctor I wanted my tubes tied, and there was a new procedure that hit the market for sterilization. An instrument inserted into the fallopian tubes would create scar tissue that would develop, causing the sterilization. The morning of my procedure, my mom came over to watch the kids. Sean was supposed to take me to the hospital to have the procedure. Instead, he got up that morning and left for work. That morning, he decided he did not want to participate in the process. It didn't take long before I had my fifth child.

Having four kids meant that I was a stay-at-home mom for the most part. I never envisioned myself as a stay-at-home mom, but it made the most sense with the cost of childcare. I decided to be the best homemaker I knew how to be. I was often exhausted, but I took pride in being able to teach my children. I tried to create an environment where I was attentive and truly involved with them. I appreciated the ability to volunteer at the schools and essentially be a great soccer mom. I drew heavily on my motherhood to provide me with a sense of purpose. As much as I tried to create the environment, I very much hoped of raising my children in, it wasn't enough to sustain the family built on trauma and dysfunction. The harder I tried to be perfect, the more I hated myself for falling short. Trying to keep up appearances was exhausting, but I wanted to keep up the facade of a perfectly, well taken care of family.

Reactions to protect yourself, can sometimes suffocate your ability to stay in tune with who you truly are. When survival becomes the goal, we often lose sight of our deeper selves, buried beneath the defense mechanisms we've built to cope with harsh realities. Over time, succumbing to the environment around you, you start to allow your situation to define not just your limits but your potential. It's as if the weight of your circumstances dictates your worth and your capacity to thrive.

In those moments, the lack of empowerment is very present. You can feel powerless as if life is happening around you and you're simply a passenger, hoping to make it through. You become out of touch with the understanding that you are, in fact, in control of your circumstances. Instead of recognizing your agency, you become confined by the narrative that has been placed upon you,the belief that your current situation is all you're capable of, that your survival is the best you can hope for.

But the truth is, survival is only the first step. It's not the destination. We often get stuck in survival mode, thinking that making it through the day, the year, and the crisis is all that life has to offer. In that place, we forget that we were meant for so much more than just getting by. We forget that we have the power to create, to transform, and to transcend whatever situation we are in. Our circumstances do not define us, however, our response to them does.

When you come to understand that you are more than your survival instincts, you begin to reclaim the narrative. You shift from merely existing to fully living. This shift requires courage, the courage to acknowledge that while survival may have kept you safe, it has also kept you small. To rise above survival and to thrive, you must step into the truth that you are capable of reshaping your circumstances. You are not helpless. You are not at the mercy of your environment. You have the power to rewrite the script, to step out of the shadow of survival and into the light of possibility. Empowerment is not just about knowing your strength; it's about reconnecting with the part of you that is capable of more than you ever imagined. It's about recognizing that the power to shape your life was always within you, even when survival felt like your only option. Once you awaken to this realization, you stop allowing life to happen to you and start making life happen for you.

Independence Day

I thought I could wait it out. I figured I could leave once my kids got older or once the violence stopped. The infidelity seemed to have stopped. We moved to a beautiful home closer to my parents just before I gave birth to my youngest child. It seemed like life was adjusting, and things settled down between us. That didn't last long, though. Sean's decision to "do the right thing" and be a loving husband came with a deep darkness that created an ambient fear in our home. That sounds contradictory, I know, but him being more present at home meant there were more opportunities for him to be upset about the slightest things. I always felt like he resented me for having children, being his wife, hell, resented me for existing. No matter how hard I tried to make him happy, I couldn't. I lost all sense of self-identity. I did not have my own thoughts nor opinions. I didn't know where he ended, and I began. My identity mirrored his being. I was only an extension of him; his wife. The mother of HIS children. The object of his frustration.

I saw that he was deeply unhappy and turning to religion to soothe his soul. I don't know if he clung to church in an effort to tame the demons that weighed him down. What I do know is that he became extremely self-righteous. He was one of those church people who would condescendingly spew scripture at you but never quite lived the life he preached about. That was extremely confusing to me. About every six months, he would have this deep revelation about how he was not actually saved and on certain Sundays, he would rededicate his life to Jesus. I came to the realization that this was just who he was. Not a million hours of prayer or a hundred alter calls was going to change this man. Being a "good wife," I made sure to ask the nurse to make notes about asking him about depression during his doctor visits. That was another attempt of me to excuse his behavior and blame it on something else. His parents, his sex addiction, and his depression. His answer to all things, was prayer. Now, I believe in prayer, but if I were diagnosed with cancer, I am going to get treatment of some kind while I pray. The same approach should be taken for mental health.

Sean took a trip to Atlanta for his cousin's wedding in 2013. When he came back, something had shifted. He was even more distant, cruel, and intolerant of me, like a part of him had finally detached from our life as a family. I remember feeling utterly hopeless, like I was standing on the edge of a cliff, waving frantically for him to see me, to hear me, but he was already gone. One night, during an argument, I broke down. Desperate for him to understand how deeply his words and actions were cutting me, I said something I'd never thought I'd say: "I want to kill myself."

Without hesitation, he yelled back, "Well, do it then!"

His words hung in the air like a challenge, sharp and cruel, hitting me harder than any insult or accusation he'd thrown before. I was stunned by his indifference but even more by the fact that part of me started to consider it. I really thought about how I could end it all; how I could escape the pain.

Would it be pills? I opened the medicine cabinet one night, staring blankly at the bottles, trying to figure out which ones and how many would be enough to stop the ache inside. I imagined the silence that would follow, the relief from the constant, throbbing pain in my heart.

As I closed the cabinet, I caught sight of my boys standing behind me, their wide eyes looking up at me with curiosity and innocence. In that moment, my heart shattered. How could I ever leave them? How could I abandon my children. They looked to me for love and protection? But that didn't stop the darkness from creeping in at night when the house was quiet, and all I had left were my thoughts. Some nights, the ache was so unbearable that I would lie in bed, staring at the ceiling, praying for God to let me die in my sleep. I begged Him to stop my heart from beating so I wouldn't have to face another day of feeling unseen, unwanted, and broken.

But every morning, my heart kept beating. God didn't answer

my prayer in the way that I thought I wanted. Each day that I woke up, there was a reminder that there was still a purpose for me, even if I couldn't see it yet. My children needed me, and somewhere deep inside, I needed me too, I just had to find that strength again.

In April 2014, Sean and I were invited to one of my friend's weddings—my homegirl I went to high school with. To this day, my parents live a few houses down from her mom. He didn't want to go to the wedding, and on that day, he was angry with me for absolutely no reason. Looking back, maybe he felt uncomfortable being around people he didn't know. I just wanted to be there and celebrate with my friend. As much as I tried to tune him out, he ruined the experience.

As the beautiful couple exchanged vows and the pastor gave them a lovely message of encouragement, I knew then that my marriage was over. I did not have, nor have I ever had, the love they spoke about. We were thrusted into this trauma bond and tried to survive through it. On the way home, Sean threatened to put me out of the car. "Why?" I asked. He was frustrated with my disappointment of having to leave the wedding because he was uncomfortable. If I was anything less than accommodating and agreeable, I was asked to leave the home, pack my bags, or get out of the car. Anything to show dominance and power.

As things continued to escalate in our home, I found an outlet through social media. I joined a support group for co-dependents on Facebook. Sean picked up a second job, so I had time to read a lot. They had articles and conversations about things like abuse and co-dependency. I knew I was co-dependent because it is something that came up in therapy. It was even a topic I heard when going through marital counseling with Sean's sex addiction sponsor. There was a woman in the Facebook group with whom I became friends. She was married to a pastor with many of the same traits as Sean. We shared stories, and for once,

I didn't feel alone. The research I did, in addition to reading blogs and books, really empowered me. I felt like there were other people in my situation. Putting a name to what I was experiencing allowed me to navigate through the complicated relationship that I had.

My sister-in-law, Brianna, found herself in an abusive relationship, and we ended up talking about our similar experiences. She was truly a safe person for me to confide in about what life was like in my home. I started to share my desire to leave with Brianna. She cautioned me not to tell him I was leaving. She reminded me that letting him know my next move could cause me harm. We had a safe word so that she knew that it was me texting or emailing her. She was one of my biggest allies. She grew up with Sean and knew exactly what he was capable of. It gave me a sense of relief because I loved Sean's family so much. I didn't want to lose them if I left. Brianna was one of the only available friends I had at that time to lean on.

Detachment. That is what saved me. I read somewhere in my scouring through the internet that detachment was the best way to survive in abusive relationships. So, I detached. I had a part-time job on the weekends working at a nursing home from 3-11pm. I tried to make sure the house was in order, and the kids were taken care of before I left. That wasn't always possible.

During the downward spiral toward the end of our marriage, I cared less and less about trying to be perfect. I went to work one evening and didn't make dinner for the family before I left for the night. I got a call while I was making my rounds with residents from Sean. "Why didn't you make dinner!?" "Sean, all of the ingredients to make spaghetti, are in the cabinet." I tried to reason with him. He yelled through the phone. I just simply asked him, "Why are you so angry?" His response was, "You goofy, chick" as he hung up the phone.

When I got home that night, he continued to express his frustration. He called me an "idiot" when I came through the door to find the poorly made dinner and messy kitchen. He probably felt bad for not knowing how to cook and projected that onto me. My oldest was there listening. Normally I would've cried and pitifully asked him to stop. But the detached me just looked at him. Then, I looked at my son and said, "It is not okay for anyone to talk to someone like that." Things continued to escalate the more I detached from him. I had a conversation with my then five-year-old the day after he saw his father choke me and threaten to kill me for not washing the dishes. He innocently said, "I was sad because if he killed you, who would take care of us?" He told me that he thought his dad was sorry because he bought me flowers that day. I was disgusted at what my children were seeing. I talked to Sean about going back to counseling together, and he felt like our past attempts didn't work. He expressed that he was just tired of trying. I asked if he wanted to separate. He didn't like my suggestion to leave him. He told me that no one would want me with four kids. Maybe that was his plan. He always reminded me that I was nothing without him.

I ended up going to counseling by myself. I knew that I needed help. For the first time, I was completely honest about the years of abuse and infidelity. Something in me snapped. I listened to myself and actually sat in the reality that I let this happen to me. It was disturbing to hear myself talk about the life I was living out loud. Not the life I portrayed, but the reality of what it was. To look at the empathetic face of my therapist and realize how deeply I had sunken into this dark place of misery and self-loathing, was awakening.

On July 4th, 2014, we visited Sean's mother. He went over from time to time to help her cut the grass. We were coming to the end of our lease, and he asked me to contact the property manager about renewing the lease. I wasn't able to do that before the holiday. He threw a fit on his mother's front lawn. She intervened and asked him to stop throwing a tantrum. He relaxed for the time being, but when we got home, he continued to badger me. I tried to leave the house as I felt him becoming more aggressive. Before I could get through the door, he ran to slam my body in the doorway. He always told me to leave but never actually let me go. I ended up bruised and in pain from being shut in the door. He then took my keys and phone away. I decided to go to my room feeling defeated. At that time, I just started a new job working the overnight shift at the hospital where my mom worked. I thought I'd try to take a nap before going to work, but he wouldn't let me sleep.I got up and went to work that night. I did not want to go back home once my shift was over.

Everything I had was there, and my children were there, but I did not want to go back. Several weeks before this, I posed a question to my Facebook group about how to leave a situation like this. Someone told me about a friend who just decided enough was enough and just walked away. That didn't resonate with me. I had nothing to stand on. No money of my own. I never had anything in my name, so I had no credit. I just lived in his shadow, so how could I survive with four children? I came up with a plan. I was going to go to nursing school while I worked nights. I took the entrance exam and was ready to start. The other part of my plan was to apply for a credit card to establish credit for myself.

I had it all planned out. My exit strategy was to gain my independence so I could stand on my own and raise my children. I grew up watching my aunts struggle as single parents, and I feared that the most. For nine years, my mom raised me by herself. I almost feared being a single mother more than I feared Sean's temper. I left before, but at that time I didn't want to face that struggle of single motherhood. Feeling like I had nothing and nowhere to go made me go back. Not that night, though. As I worked in the Medical Observation Unit during the July 4th holiday, I reached my breaking point. Suddenly, what that woman said about knowing you've had enough made sense.

I got off work the next morning and went to my parent's house instead of going home. I had to tell my parents what had been going on for the last several years. They didn't understand why I didn't say anything. By the time Sean realized I wasn't coming back home, he cut off my access to our bank account. Then, he cut off my phone. The more he showed his ass, the less I had any desire to go back. In that moment I made a declaration—he was never going to hurt me again. And so, that was the last time I would live in that house with him.

Part 3

The Return with Wisdom

The mud that the Lotus fights through to blossom does not attach itself to the beautiful flower. Through rooted darkness, the lotus rises strongly toward the sun and slowly opens up unscathed by the weight it pushes through to bloom for all the world to see. Many look to the flower as a symbol of resilience and strength. To bloom like the lotus is to embrace the process. It is to acknowledge that the mud, though unpleasant, plays a role in our transformation. It is to realize that beauty and strength can coexist,that we can rise from the darkness and still stand tall, unscathed by what we've endured, ready to show the world the strength and beauty that have been within us all along.

The Safe House

My therapist and I meticulously crafted a safety plan. Each step designed to guide me toward freedom and security. Years ago, my first therapist as an adult, emphasized the importance of leaving a paper trail. "Even if you're not ready to press charges," she advised, "always make a report." She understood the gravity of the abuse I was enduring and knew that documentation could one day be my lifeline. She suggested simple yet crucial measures, like leaving an extra key to my car hidden somewhere accessible and being prepared to exit swiftly if necessary.

Now, eight years later, with the support of another dedicated therapist, I had an exit strategy I was finally ready to execute. The façade I had maintained of a happy family life had crumbled. The part of me that had suppressed my true feelings for so long was irreparably broken. I no longer had the capacity or the will to endure the endless cycle of abuse and reconciliation. It was time to reclaim my life.

My therapist provided me with a wealth of resources tailored for women who had suffered through domestic violence. Among them were several organizations I was already familiar with, including one I had sought help from years before we got married. That particular shelter was a sprawling mansion with numerous rooms dedicated to women and their children seeking refuge. I vividly remember meeting a woman that I will never forget. We met in the common area where everyone came to watch TV. She was in a wheelchair with a broken leg. I sat with her and she told about how her husband brutally attacked her. As she detailed her story—trying to get the words out through her wired broken jaw, I wondered if I truly belonged in a place like that. "Sure, he choked me," I rationalized, "but at least he didn't break my jaw." With that misguided reasoning, I left the safety of the mansion and returned to him, never imagining that things could escalate to that same horrifying level, until they did, and my own ankle was fractured. Because of shame I couldn't identify how potentially dangerous my situation could get. I was reluctant to tap into the many resources available. There were times I even chose to sleep in my car rather than let anyone know what I was going through.

One of the layered complexities of domestic violence is how challenging it is to walk away from the relationship. It can take some women up to seven or eight times of leaving and going back in domestic violence situations, before they leave for good.

A few weeks before I finally left, I reached out to the domestic violence shelter. I spoke to the hotline operator, detailing how my husband had recently threatened to burn me with an iron because I hadn't ironed his clothes. I explained that as I continued to emotionally disconnect, his threats were becoming more severe. I believed he sensed his grasp on control was weakening as I was secretly planning my exit. To compensate, he escalated his use of fear and intimidation.

Detecting hesitation in my voice, the operator gently suggested that I might not be entirely ready to be taken in by the shelter. She encouraged me to continue therapy and to keep reaching out.

I went on to tell her that when the threat of being burned didn't get a reaction from me, he amped up. I explained what prompted me to call the hotline that day: In a fit of rage, he ordered our children to bring up our suitcases from the basement and into our bedroom. One by one, he packed all my belongings, what didn't fit in the suitcases, he shoved into garbage bags.

"Get out of my house," he demanded, frantically pulling my clothes from hangers.

I didn't want any violence, so I complied. The last time I had matched his energy, I ended up with a broken ankle. So, I chose to obey, hoping he would eventually exhaust himself. But my emotional detachment only seemed to fuel his rage.

He loaded my things into the van along with the kids. Then, he went back into the house while I sat in the front seat, looking at my children fastened in their car seats behind me. I had no idea where we were going. When he returned, he sat down, slipped his handgun into the side pocket of the driver's door, and started the engine.

Is he going to shoot me in front of my kids?

Part of me knew he was using every tool of intimidation he had left. But another part of me grew nervous about how far he was willing to take this. I didn't want to play his game anymore.

We pulled up to a homeless shelter where he worked part-time. Still, I had no reaction. I had nothing left to give him, no begging, no pleading, no fear to feed his control. At that moment, if pulling the trigger would set me free, I was willing to accept it.

I recounted our history and my growing fears to the operator. I wanted to leave, but I was affraid of what might happen if I took that step. The operator's words lingered with me in the days that followed, and my resolve strengthened. When I called the shelter again, I was ready. They directed me to a confidential location, a safe house whose address I had to promise never to disclose. Much like the shelter I had visited years before, it was a large, welcoming house filled with several rooms. I was assigned a spacious room with enough beds for me and my children, and we shared the space with a Polish woman and her young daughter. Despite the language barrier, we found common ground in watching our children play together; their laughter transcending any need for words.

The house was alive with the sounds of children, their playful energy bringing lightness to an otherwise heavy atmosphere. They ran freely in the backyard playground, their joy a reminder of resilience in the midst of adversity. The shelter provided all of our meals, and each mother was assigned specific responsibilities to contribute to our communal living. We participated in group therapy sessions on designated days, and each of us worked individually with a counselor to develop a plan for life after our six-week stay. To my surprise and relief, my children adored the safe house. They formed fast friendships and created cherished memories through endless games and adventures. Even after we moved on, they would often ask if we could return, associating the place with happiness and security. For me, the night we arrived was the first time in years I felt a profound sense of relief wash over me. I had finally broken free. Alone in our room that first night, I put on my headphones, let the music fill the space, and wept tears of joy. I danced around the room, celebrating my newfound freedom and strength until exhaustion put me to sleep.

Throughout this period, I maintained my job at the hospital, working night shifts to support my family. My parents were incredibly supportive, taking care of the kids while I worked. They knew about our situation at the shelter, but with limited space in their home, they couldn't accommodate all five of us immediately. My stepdad, began to take everything out of his office to eventually make room for us, but until then, the shelter was our sanctuary.

My mother offered words of wisdom that became my mantra during this time: "Do not feel sorry for yourself. Get dressed every day and carry yourself like you won't be there long." Taking her advice to heart, I dressed professionally each day, projecting confidence and determination. Every time we left the shelter, I packed all our belongings into suitcases and loaded them into my car. I refused to let myself get too comfortable, constantly reminding myself that this was a temporary chapter in our lives.

I filed for separation at the courthouse, initiating the formal process to dissolve our marriage. Despite everything, I didn't prevent Sean from seeing the kids. Initially, he attempted to coerce me back through intimidation, but when that failed, he tried to woo me with incessant phone calls and unsolicited gifts, like flowers sent to my parents' home. We arranged to exchange the children at the police station for safety, but his erratic behavior remained unsettling.

One particular exchange at the station stands out vividly in my memory. Sean tried to reminisce, saying, "I remember when you were just fifteen..." I cut him off sharply, "Just stop. I don't want to hear that." His demeanor shifted instantly from faux nostalgia to palpable anger, like a malfunctioning robot switching modes. I couldn't shake the feeling that if he ever got close enough, he would try to seriously hurt me. My fears weren't unfounded.

On another occasion, I arranged to meet Sean to exchange the kids and collect some necessary paperwork. I brought my mom along, believing her presence would deter any hostile behavior. I was wrong. A heated exchange of words between him and my mother escalated quickly. Unable to direct his aggression toward her, he turned on me instead,grabbing my shirt, throwing me to the ground, and slamming me with a car door. I filed a police report immediately, and due to the visible bruises and torn clothing, charges were pressed without delay. This incident prompted me to file an order of protection against him.

One of the most invaluable resources provided by the shelter was access to a law firm specializing in domestic violence cases. They worked pro bono, offering the legal support I desperately needed but couldn't afford. With their guidance, I navigated the complex processes of establishing a custody agreement and finalizing the divorce. It was a problematic two-year battle of endless court appearances and negotiations. Still, I was determined to see it through for the sake of my children and myself.

Sean's desperation to locate us intensified. He enlisted friends and family to call me, attempting to extract information about our whereabouts. One afternoon, as the kids and I were headed to my parent's house, we were involved in a car accident caused by a young man making an illegal turn. The van needed repairs, and while notifying the insurance company, Sean was called by the company and made aware of the repair process. Seizing the opportunity, he went to the collision repair shop, demanded they stop all work and forcibly took the van. The mechanic called me and told me that Sean demanded they reattach the damaged pieces of the van. He didn't waste any time. He combed through the navigation system and let me know that he discovered the address of the safe house, compromising our security.

In this challenging time, a neighbor and friend of my family graciously lent me her car so I could continue commuting to work. Her kindness was a godsend, a reminder that people are willing to offer light even in darkness. My lawyer successfully petitioned the judge to include the van in the order of protection, ensuring I had rightful access to transportation. Nevertheless, Sean defied the order once more by retaking the van, resulting in his arrest for violating the protection order. His chilling words echoed in my mind: "An order of protection is just a piece of paper. If I wanted to do something to you, I could just come up to your job." The threat hung heavy in the air, and I lived each day with a lingering sense of unease, never fully feeling safe.

Finally, my parents completed the necessary adjustments to their home, and we moved in with them. My stepdad had cleared out his office, making space for all five of us to share two beds in a room, no bigger than a medium sized bathroom, on the lower level of their home. Despite the highly cramped space, I was immensely grateful to be surrounded by family.

At the shelter, we had to sign in and out every time we left, specifying our return times, which felt very restrictive. When asked what time we'd return on our last day there, I confidently wrote, "NEVER." At that moment, I declared to myself and the universe that I would never again find myself living in a shelter.

Leaving the safe house marked the beginning of a new chapter in our lives, a journey toward healing, independence, and rediscovering joy.

New Beginnings

Sean tried tirelessly to get custody of our children, using everything in his power to discredit me as a mother. The death of our son was weaponized, and it continued to be for years to come. His relentless need for control drove his actions, though perhaps at first, he believed that having custody would force me to come back. In court, his angle was that I lived in my parent's basement, the five of us, in one room. The argument was that I was unable to care for the children in those conditions.

He even convinced his mother to call me, pressuring me to give him the children. "What are you going to do? You're homeless!" she passionately expressed. It was exceptionally disturbing because she was one of the first people I turned to when I left. I sat beside her, on her bed, explaining why I had to go. She had once told me she disagreed with her son's behavior, saying, "That's too much control for one person to have over someone else." There was a part of me that wanted her blessing, some validation that I wasn't crazy for leaving. I needed her approval, and for some reason, I trusted her. In the past, she was one of the few who could call Sean out on his behavior, and he would listen. So, there were times I kept her in the loop, thinking she might help.

Sean's relationship with his mother was complicated. It was filled with a strange mix of yearning for her love and guidance, alongside deep-seated resentment and disrespect. I could only imagine the guilt trip he placed on her, turning her from an ally for me into yet another extension of his abuse. She even went so far as to tell me that if I divorced Sean, biblically, I could never remarry. Sean was a master manipulator skilled at altering perceptions and twisting reality to fit his narrative.

When the issue of my living conditions came up in court, the judge looked at my lawyer and asked, "When are we going to write up a motion for possession of the marital home?" That day, I was told that my children and I could move back into the house, and Sean would have to leave. My initial response was relief, but then doubt started to creep in. Could I afford to maintain the home? And more importantly, would I be safe from Sean? My mom and I sat at the dinner table, writing down expenses, trying to figure out how much money I'd need to sustain the home. Just as we were calculating the numbers, I received a call.

While in the shelter, I applied to various organizations that assisted with housing, one of which was Christian Charities. They provided subsidized housing for families experiencing homelessness. "Hello," I answered the call. On the other end was, Violet, the caseworker who had been working tirelessly to find us a home. Her voice was heavy with a thick, cheerful Nigerian accent as she said, "We have found a place for you and your children." She went on to describe the two-bedroom apartment she had secured for us. God's timing was impeccable. Violet's kind heart and exceptional work not only provided us with a home but also offered sage advice on how to use this time wisely. "Work hard and save your money," she said.

Violet had explained that it was difficult to find a place for us because most townships required a three-bedroom living space for a family of five. But she found a township where that limitation was not enforced. And so, Elk Grove Village became our new home. On Christmas Eve 2014, my kids and I sat in our empty apartment, with a sparsely decorated artificial pine tree standing proudly in the middle of the furnitureless living room. The joy I felt was overwhelming. Being able to be in my own space with my children was incredibly rewarding and freeing. Every time I pulled up and took my key out to unlock the door, I felt a deep sense of pride. Things were finally coming together.

Everything I had worried about was resolving in ways that could only be explained by a higher power watching over me, orchestrating every step. Doors were opening, clarity was emerging, and my faith in God grew stronger.

Yet, as I faced the finalization of my divorce, I found myself deeply conflicted. Growing up in a religious household, I had been taught that marriage was sacred, a lifelong bond that wasn't to be broken. The church was the foundation of family, stability, and faith. Walking away from my marriage felt like walking away from that foundation; a kind of exile from everything I had known. Divorce wasn't just a separation from my husband. It felt like a separation from my faith, from God Himself.

The marriage itself had become a prison, trapping me in a cycle of pain that was spiritually and emotionally crushing. The weight of my husband's control and the distorted version of faith I had been living left me feeling like I had no voice, no choice but to submit and endure. It was as if I had to sacrifice my own spirit to uphold the ideas I was taught. The longer I stayed, the more I realized that I was suffocating under the guise of religious duty.

In the process of making that decision, I wrestled with guilt and shame, questioning if I was forsaking God by stepping away. As I distanced myself from that version of faith, something beautiful began to unfold. For the first time, I felt God's presence with a different kind of closeness; not through the doctrines I had grown up with, but in a gentler, more intimate way.

I found that God was not punishing or abandoning me. Instead, I sensed Him guiding me with a kind of love and understanding I had rarely felt within the confines of that marriage. It was as though He was reassuring me that this path was not one of sin, but one of survival and self-rediscovery. I realized I didn't have to sever my faith to seek freedom and healing; instead, I had to step out of the rigid rules that had kept me bound to believe that suffering was synonymous with holiness.

In those moments, I felt God's hand over my life more than ever, guiding me to trust that I was walking a path of purpose, one where I could honor Him without losing myself.

I made our little second-floor apartment as cozy as I could. My parents helped me furnish it, and I tried my best to make it feel like home. The kids, having no concept of what an apartment was, thought it was like the safe house. They quickly had to learn that they couldn't run up and down the hallways as they had before. The boys took the master bedroom while my daughter and I shared the other room. My then three-year-old son often slept in my room. Many nights, all four children crowded into my bed. Squished but safe and secure, we finally had a place to call our own.

There were times I missed my old life and even questioned if I missed Sean, or at least some of the good times we had. The road ahead was going to be difficult, and I often wondered if I was capable of handling it all. I had two years of assistance from Christian Charities, then, I would have to pay the $1,260 rent on my own after graduating the program.

My little appartment was about 20 minutes from my parents. Now that I was in my own place, working the night shift was no longer feasible, without convieniently having help of my family. Leaving the kids with my parents at night was easy when we lived with them, but it became more of a hassle than it was helpful. I placed the kids in daycare, left my job at the hospital, and started working day shifts with a home health agency run by friends I had met when I was 19.

One of my favorite clients was an elderly man named Mitch, who lived in a retirement community. He had suffered a stroke that left him without the use of the left side of his body. I would visit him for a few hours each day, ensuring I could pick up the kids from daycare on time. The flexibility allowed me to be there for my children, but it wasn't enough money. After the two-year order of protection was lifted, Sean's first move was to take the van. I could only borrow a car for so long.

These adjustments were especially hard for Isaiah, who, at eight years old, was old enough to understand what was happening. He took on a lot of his father's emotions during that time, and the dramatic departure from the life he once knew caused him to act out a lot. One day, he had a complete meltdown over a basketball he had left in the van. He kicked and screamed; it was almost unbearable. At that moment, I remembered something his therapist told me: Isaiah's acting out was an outward expression of his need to know that he could have these big emotions and that I could handle it and still love him.

There were times when I honestly couldn't handle it. My own mental capacity was stretched thin, but this day, I had the strength. While he kicked and screamed about the ball, I grabbed him from behind and held him tightly. He kicked and screamed a bit longer, yelling, "I want my ball back!" I just told him that I loved him while I embraced him. "I just want things to be how they used to be," he eventually calmed down, curling up in my lap and weeping softly. I cried with him, saying, "Sometimes I do too." I had to validate his feelings, understanding that none of the children could make such a drastic and sudden adjustment without experiencing painful and unfamiliar emotions.

Every time the thought of missing my old life crossed my mind, Sean would do or say something so outrageous that I was reminded why I left. It was as if God was showing me that my old life was nothing more than a façade; a toxic trap that I had finally escaped. I missed the idea of having a family and the desire not to raise my children in a broken home. I missed the conveniences of never worrying about bills or grocery money, but I knew that mindset was what had kept me in a toxic marriage for so long. I had to let it go and accept my new normal. It wasn't glamorous. I struggled. I was stressed. But I was also free.

In those first months, I had to hold on to the anger to keep myself from going back. I needed that fire, that raw pain, to remind me why I left and to push me forward. It was like my mind needed a shock to break the patterns of loyalty that had kept me bound for so long. My instinct, born from years of trauma, was to bury the hurt, to pretend it didn't sting so much. Suppressing pain was second nature to me,a survival skill I'd developed to keep going in the face of relentless challenges. This time, I forced myself to sit with the uncomfortable feelings. I allowed myself to feel the betrayal, the disappointment, and the sorrow. It was a kind of armor, a necessary layer of protection.

Holding on to the pain gave me the strength to detach, to remember why going back wasn't an option. But as time went on, I could feel that anger hardening, turning from a shield into a weight. It threatened to make me bitter, clouding my spirit and weighing down my heart. When I noticed that bitterness taking root, I knew it was time to let go.

Eventually, I released that anger because I didn't want it to define me nor to shape the new life I was building. I wanted to move forward with a spirit of hope, not resentment. But in those early days, that anger was a lifeline,a reminder of my strength and the fuel to keep pressing forward, even when the road felt endless.

In one of my sessions, my therapist created a bridge on an easel with a giant notebook attached. She asked me to list what I was leaving behind,not just leaving Sean, but what about my life I wanted to change. I listed things like feeling afraid, never feeling good enough, abuse, and manipulation. Then, she asked me where I was going,not a physical place, but what I wanted out of life. I listed happiness, autonomy, peace, love, and so on. The space between what I was leaving and where I was going represented the steps I needed to take to get there. I had to get a full-time job, continue therapy, and find my voice in the court process. This thought process not only shaped my life during this transition but also became a fundamental approach for me in life. Where do I want to go? Who do I have to become to get there? I had taken the first steps toward achieving the life I wanted.

Once the order of protection was lifted, discussions about establishing a parenting schedule began. Finally, the judge reached a conclusion, and our divorce was finalized after a long two years of litigation. We had no joint assets and no money to dispute over. We spent those two years in a power struggle over custody of the children. The judge described the case as one of the worst he'd ever seen. The day I left was the day I was done with the marriage, but throughout those long two years, I often questioned my decision. In hindsight, it seems obvious to leave, but when you've never had a voice, you constantly question your ability to make choices for your life. I had to learn how to trust myself to make the right decisions for my life and for my children. The judge granted 50/50 parenting time. When it went into effect, I had a challenging time without my children. It was something I had to get used to. It was a part of the new normal.

As my time with Christian Charities drew to a close, I faced a critical decision: What would be my next move? I had managed to save a decent amount of money, but as a former stay-at-home mom, I hadn't fully anticipated the overwhelming cost of childcare and summer camp. My savings wouldn't last long. To make matters worse, I needed a car to get around. I sent out my resume and, by sheer chance, received a call from a place I hadn't even applied to, a growing hospice company that needed CNAs to travel across the Chicagoland area, caring for patients. The thought of taking care of people on their deathbeds wasn't ideal, especially given my grim association with death, but the money and flexibility were hard to resist. I accepted the position, took my offer letter to a car dealership, and bought a car.

I was paid per visit and had to travel extensively, all the while keeping in mind that I needed to pick up my children from daycare by 6 p.m. The job pushed me to perfect my craft, allowing me to efficiently visit all my patients and still be on time for my kids. I wanted each of my patients and their families to feel truly cared for. The owners of the hospice company often said, "You don't choose hospice,hospice chooses you." It was more than a job; it was a calling. Over time, I came to believe that being a caregiver in any capacity is indeed a calling. Being with people at the end of their lives was transformative. Many times, I was sent to care for someone, but it was I who gained the most from those experiences.

After losing a child, my perspective on life changed drastically. The depth of love and compassion I felt for all people grew exponentially. Working in hospice forced me to confront death in ways I never imagined I could. Each home I entered was a new experience, and working in hospice meant caring for not just the patient but their family as well. Often, the patient was unable to communicate, so I spent much of my time talking with their loved ones. I became skilled at recognizing the signs of the end of life: decreased breathing, a slower heart rate, and mottled skin, especially around the toes and feet. These were difficult conversations to have, but they were necessary. There was also wisdom to be gained from these challenging moments.

I vividly remember the first time I watched someone make the transition. It was Christmas Day 2015, my first Christmas without my children. The administration sent out a text asking for volunteers to be sitters, someone to sit with a patient for hours, usually in the final stages of life. I figured I might as well go; it would give the family a break to enjoy the holiday and give me a sense of purpose. The elderly gentleman I sat with lived in a nursing home. Hours went by as I repositioned him to ensure his comfort and took his vitals every hour. Eventually, his breathing became sparse, and I could barely detect a pulse. Then, his breathing stopped altogether.

I made the necessary calls and notified the nursing home staff. I cleaning the body and waited for his family to arrive. His son came in and thanked me for being there. He sat next to his father on the bed. "You know," He began to share his thoughts about his father's death. "It would've been better if he would've died from a heart attack or something." He shared how his father had suffered from dementia and how, in a way, they had lost him long before his death. It had been painful for the family to watch him slowly deteriorate over the years.

The nurse came to relieve me, I left, sat in my car, and wept. I had managed to keep it together for the family, but alone, a flood of emotions hit me. My brain connected the lifeless body before me to the day I held my son for the last time. I was overcome with sorrow and grief, doubting if I could continue in this line of work. The next day, I was recognized for my sacrifice, which gave me the strength to hold onto the sense of purpose I had found. Over time, I grew to love my job. It became more than just a paycheck, it felt like the calling everyone spoke of. There was a profound love cultivated for the elderly, a connection that transcended age.

There was a time I covered for another hospice aide and took over her route for the week. One of her patients, Mrs. Lola, called the office and specifically requested that I be her permanent aide. She lived in an apartment far from my usual route, but I made it work. Apart from my accommodating nature, I felt it was simply the right thing to do. Mrs. Lola didn't require much; she still got around quite well initially. She just wanted someone to sit and talk with her, and so we did. We talked about everything, her life, current events, our children. Mrs. Lola had lost a son, just like I had. Though we didn't say much about our losses, there was a deep sense of connection between us.

As the weeks passed, Mrs. Lola's condition worsened, and she became bedridden. Our lively conversations ceased, replaced by a gentle presence. One day, I received a call from Mrs. Lola's daughter. "It's Mom's time," she gently let me know that I no longer needed to come visit. She expressed her gratitude for the care I had provided and mentioned that her mother often spoke of me. Before we ended the call, she asked, "What was your son's name who passed away?" I told her, "Demetrius." She repeated his name, then said, "I'll tell Mom to give him a big hug and kiss for you when she makes it up there." Her words were the biggest gift she could have given me. I don't know how things work on the other side of this life, but that gave me hope. I imagined that every person I cared for who made the transition was another hug and kiss from me to heaven.

Despite my love for my work, I knew I couldn't do it forever. The physical demands were taking a toll on my body, and I began to experience chronic back pain. I often crossed paths with the marketers from my company. They were always dressed sharply, exuding confidence. I started to picture myself trading in my scrubs for a well-tailored suit. That became my next career goal. I shared my ambitions with my colleagues, and they encouraged me to go for it. As I continued my education, working toward a degree, my confidence soared. I decided to approach the Director of Business Development,who was also the CEO's wife,and ask for a position on her team. They had already praised my work ethic and positioned me as a leader to train other aides. I figured it was a good time to make my move.

She told me to start connecting with the other marketers and providing information about potential new patients. I was becoming part of the marketing team. However, as the company grew, the need for quality care outweighed the need for new marketers. I realized I had to leave the company to be fully recognized for my potential.

An opportunity arose at an upscale long-term care community that would be life-changing. My cousin and I always worked together in some capacity. She had worked at the group home with me while studying to become a nurse, then at the hospice company. Eventually, she became a Director of Nursing at an assisted living community. It seemed only fitting that I would join her in administration. There was an opening for an Assistant Executive Director, and I saw it as a chance to make a real difference in healthcare. With years of experience as an aide and my growing knowledge of business management, I applied for the position. My cousin got me the interview and armed me with inside information, I was able to present a solution to a staffing issue they had been struggling with.

I got the job, and it was the highest-paying position I had ever held. I was in a leadership role with the opportunity to learn about all aspects of operations. I wore many hats, HR, scheduling, marketing, training, recruiting, payroll, and anything else that needed managing. It was a huge responsibility, but I loved it. I was able to make an impact not only on the residents but also on the employees.

Being a leader meant I had the ability to change lives in a way that I encountered during my journey to self-sufficiency. I intentionally sought out individuals who needed that one open door. There were so many people who guided me along the way—it only made sense to take that opportunity to do the same for others.

My position allowed me to be, not only a leader, but a mentor. I trained young women and men on how to provide care for the residents in the community. I didn't just sit in my office and make demands, I worked side by side teaching and developing my staff. Those hours of training weren't just about job responsibilities, they were opportunities to have conversations with the young people I hired. We talked about career aspirations, and I even found myself problem-solving personal challenges.

I had one young woman who seemed ambitious, full of energy with a true desire to take care of others. Her eagerness to work and learn, dissipated and she became unreliable. I was getting frustrated with her new behavior until she came to work trying to hide her bruised face. When I asked her about the bruise, she didn't seem to want to talk about. She told me some story, but I was able to read through it. Because of our established relationship, I was able to have a private conversation about what was truly the cause of her bruises and her frequent missed days of work. My own experience allowed me to plant a seed of encouragement, in hopes that she would find her way out of a situation that was abusive.

Every part of my journey prepared me for each space I elevated to. The knowledge I gained gave me insight that I used to help those that I encountered along the way. My drive to become successful was fueled by my desire to help others.

In just four years, I had gone from being homeless with nothing more than a high school diploma to becoming an Assistant Director. I was determined to validate the idea that I was capable of achieving more. I didn't know exactly how I was going to get there, but I did know I had to be able to visualize my future. That hunger for something more, and the will to be able to make a declaration for anyone that endured what had gone through, kept me moving forward, step by step, even when the path ahead was unclear.

Photography: Solomon kelly

Transform and Transcend

In my sophomore year in high school, I had a social studies teacher who gave the class an assignment that forever resonated with me. He explained the idea of monuments representing the legacy of an individual. We were given the task of drawing a picture of what we'd want our monument to be in our remembrance. I drew a circle of stick figures joined together, hand by stick-hand, with me at the top of the circle. At the tender age of 15, I knew that I wanted my legacy to be about helping people. That is still my truth. Helping others is a part of my ethos. My hope is that anyone I am connected to in any regard is impacted in a meaningful way. In order to effectively do that, I had to take this journey of self-discovery to find my worthiness so that I would be able to help others from a place of abundance instead of a place of codependency or someone seeking validation.

If I could go back in time and talk to my 15 year-old self, I would tell her that she didn't need to look for love and validation externally. I would tell her how smart and brave she was. For as long as I can remember, I had this resounding desire to be loved and accepted and, at the same time, struggled to find myself valuable enough to be loved and accepted. Over time, I lost sight of who I was, and I wanted to become a chameleon to please everyone in an effort to fill the void I had in my heart. As time went on, I became less aware of who I was. The more tragedy I faced, the more hopeless I felt. My rock bottom was hearing my five-year-old son's fears of watching me possibly die at the hands of his father.

In the book, The Four Agreements by Don Miguel Ruiz, the author states that a person can only be abused at the level in which they abuse themselves. Why did I allow someone to treat me inhumanely? Perhaps it was because I saw no value in my own life. There was no hope for the future, only present despair. Held in my own emotional prison of self-loathing, I accepted the abuse that I had already given to myself internally. My life was a series of responses to misfortune instead of moving forward toward a goal. I got married because I lost a child. I stayed married because I made a vow to stay with the person I had children with. I froze in fear of being alone because I didn't think I was capable of thriving on my own. It wasn't until I forgave myself for the tragic accident that took my son's life, that I was able to have the clarity to strive for a life of fulfillment and joy. I believe that these lessons are given to us not only to free ourselves from the limitations of our perspective on life but also to shift the mindset of those around us. Sharing my story feels like purpose; it feels like fulfillment; it feels like destiny.

The first step toward living a fulfilled life is transforming the limiting beliefs about yourself and the world around you. Facing the hard truths about yourself is an absolutely necessary step. I had to come to terms with the fact that I allowed myself to be in an abusive relationship. Even though I was loving and accommodating, it did not mean that it would be reciprocated. While my ex-husband had his own issues he faced, I cannot hold him responsible for my life. Was he wrong? Absolutely, but acknowledging that I had control the whole time is empowering. Not at first, though. Initially, I went from trying to fix him to internalizing his actions toward me and became very ashamed. I had to learn to give myself empathy and grace. Once I was not consumed with shame and guilt, I was able to initiate my transformation.

My experiences as a child caused me to lose my voice. The ability to advocate for myself did not exist at a young age. Any sense of direction that I thought I had, was gone after losing my son. My existence only held value as a mother once I had more children. The day my child laid on the sidewalk lifeless—I, a healthcare provider, could not remember how to give CPR. I froze—and that was the state I was in for many years. That loss was the death of what little purpose I felt I had. More children came, but my confidence in being a good mother wasn't something that I desperately tried to achieve while also grappling with the intense feelings of inadequacy. Keeping them alive was the goal until I learned to embrace motherhood once again.

In accepting my position as their mom, I understood that I had to be better to myself in order to give them the best version of my ability to parent. That meant that I had to make some difficult decisions. I had to overcome what seemed damn near impossible for someone like me. Once I began to move forward and adopt the idea that I could create the life I wanted, I saw myself in a new light. Each goal I accomplished gave me more strength and courage. My faith became so strong that I believed that if something did not work out, it was not for me. Every part of my life became strategic, I no longer just let life happen. I move with intention and purpose. I learned to pivot when roadblocks came my way. Confidence is the assurance of knowing who you are. Sometimes, you have to give yourself that assurance by proving that you can accomplish the goal, overcome the fear, and believe in yourself enough to dream big.

I credit therapy in helping me find my voice. It continues to be a part of my life's journey toward healing. In every transition I face, I am grounded in the love of my family and friends. During some of the darkest times, I could rely on my small circle of loved ones to remind me that life is about collectively sharing our experiences and supporting one another. The healthiest and mutually respectful friendships, are the ones that don't require much from you. When you can just show up and be your authentic self, that is where the healing power of healthy friendships takes place. I found that friendships are as valuable as any other significant part of life. When I left my marriage, I latched on to my childhood friends and cousins. It was a refreshing reminder of who I used to be. Those are the people who give me a childlike joy and a sense of adventure. It is those relationships that still hold me accountable, keep me lifted, and provide me with encouragement. Without my circle of friends, old and new, this journey would be that much more difficult. My marriage was a bubble. I didn't have people in my life that knew me authentically. The people that surround me only knew the facade. They only saw the parts of me that I created to be accepted. I no longer have the ability to pretend.

Living freely without having to leave your authenticity behind is something I could never give up again.I've read many books on self-growth and listened to many thought leaders sharing insights on development that helped me shift my way of thinking. Understanding who I am has been my goal. My curiosity for pushing myself to achieve my highest potential has been a driving force behind gaining as much knowledge as I can. I have filled my toolbox with information that I have absorbed from the experts I admire. As life brings challenges, I have built up my toolbox with methods that could help me stay on my path toward personal growth. I've adopted a daily ritual of meditation and prayer that keeps me grounded. In my meditation, I take time to practice gratitude. This is something I've even taught to my children. Sadness and gratitude cannot coexist. Defeat and gratitude cannot coexist.

Looking forward means that goals have to be made. You cannot move toward a target that does not exist. Every year, I set goals that I want to achieve from January to December. This includes financial goals, fitness goals, spiritual goals, and adventure goals. This has helped me strive toward the things that support my ability to thrive and ultimately feel fulfilled. I have several vision boards for short-term and long-term goals. I cut out words and pictures from magazines that reflect my goals. There is something about seeing what you're aiming for that gives you the extra push.

I didn't know that there were as many resources available as I would come to know. That is a large part of why I couldn't see my way out of my darkness previously. Never let a sense of lack prevent you from believing that more is possible. There are systems set in place for those willing to help themselves.

REWRITE

THE

NARRATIVE

Part 4

The Gifts Gathered

MY TOOL BOX

In the next chapters I want to share my tool box. These are processes and ideas that I have collected throughout my years of therapy and coaching. This is how I was able to face my limiting beliefs and change the direction of my life. There will be practical steps and reflective questions. Feel free to jot down your thoughts right here in the book.

Coping Skills

One of the greatest tools I gathered through the process of my journey to find healing was learning coping skills. Given my upbringing and difficult life circumstances, living with anxiety and fighting through depression became so normal that I didn't recognize how deeply it impacted everything I did. How could I? It was ingrained in every part of my thought process from early on. It guided the decisions I made, or didn't make. It shaped my worldview and altered my perception of myself.

Coping skills are strategies and techniques used to manage emotional stress, navigate difficult situations, and regain a sense of control when life feels overwhelming. These skills aren't just helpful for surviving traumatic events; they are essential tools for approaching everyday life. For me, learning to cope started with acknowledging that something in my mental and emotional framework needed attention.

Self-Awareness

First, coping requires a sense of self-awareness. I had to identify the thought patterns and perspectives that repeatedly led me down a path of disparity. It wasn't easy, how do you detach from something that feels like it's always been a part of you? But through therapy and intentional reflection, I learned to pause and examine my thoughts instead of letting them run wild. I began to notice how certain thoughts provoked my anxiety and how the decisions I made (or avoided) were influenced by those emotions.

Self-awareness, I realized, is like turning the lights on in a dark room. Suddenly, I could see where I was stumbling, where I was holding myself back, and what was triggering my fear. From there, I could begin to use tools to diminish the impact of these thoughts on my nervous system.

Ruminating over past traumatic or painful events was something that kept me in a holding pattern. One game-changing skill I learned was mindfulness. The skill of mindfulness teaches us to stay present. Being in the present moment allowed me to sil the noise and focus on the things I do have control over. Feeling emotionally overwhelmed at times is a part of life. What I now have is the ability to journal, engage in simple things like deep breathing, or use other grounding techniques to keep me calm enough to manage my own thoughts.

Affirmation

One way to counter negative thoughts is through affirmations. Working to silence my inner critic is an ongoing process. That voice isn't nearly as loud as it had been in the past. I have learned to affirm my competence and capabilities. That is where I gained confidence to minimize the self-doubt and self-deprecating thoughts. It should truly be a daily practice for everyone.

ONCE YOU SHIFT YOUR MINDSET POSSIBILITIES OPEN UP

Mindset Shift

PRACTICAL STEPS TO SHIFT YOUR MINDSET

Changing your mindset isn't about positive thinking alone—it's about being intentional in your actions and your focus.

IDENTIFY LIMITING BELIEFS

The first step is becoming aware of the beliefs that are holding you back. Write them down, and ask yourself, "Is this true? Where did this belief come from?"

REFRAME YOUR NARRATIVE

Start rewriting the story you tell yourself. Instead of focusing on what you lack, focus on what you have. Shift from "I can't" to "How can I?"

SURROUND YOURSELF WITH GROWTH

Your environment plays a crucial role in your mindset. Surround yourself with people who encourage your growth, and create a space that supports your new vision.

PRACTICE GRATITUDE

Shifting your focus to what you're grateful for rewires your brain to see abundance instead of scarcity.

TAKE ACTION

Mindset shifts don't work without action. Start taking small steps toward your goals. With each step, your mindset will continue to evolve.

You are who you believe you are. But trying to put that together, an idea of who you are or who you could be, while in survival mode can be difficult, seemingly impossible. So, how do you begin to see yourself beyond your circumstances? Beyond merely surviving?

Processing trauma means that your brain is forced to activate fight, flight, or freeze mode. In the book, What Happened to You? by Oprah Winfrey and Dr. Bruce Perry, they explore trauma's profound effects on the brain. In the early stages of life, when your brain is highly adaptable, trauma can cause the underdevelopment of areas of your brain that are responsible for emotional regularity and executive function. These functions are responsible for how you perceive the world through your experiences and how you approach decision-making. The book looks at the ways in which you have to retrain your brain to operate from a calmer place.

In the state of survival, you are only concerned with the "right now." The immediate needs take priority over the future. The brain only has the capacity to protect itself from perceived danger and not engage in deliberate goals or plans beyond survival. New opportunities or long-term goals are not able to take root. Immediate needs take over logic and reasoning, and you are led by your emotions. I found myself reacting to feelings of anxiousness and fear throughout my life, which makes sense given my experiences. I had to rewire my thought process in order to gain a new perspective of myself and the world around me.

Many of my therapy sessions during my path to freedom gave me space to calm my reactive state of mind. We went through guided meditations where my therapist would transport me into a place of tranquility and rest. A beautiful place outside of her office where I felt peace. While my body sat on her couch, my mind escaped to that place:

Feel the weight of your body pressing into the surface beneath you. Relax your shoulders... let go of any tension in your face... unclench your jaw. Allow your arms and legs to feel heavy, grounded, and relaxed. Now, shift your attention to your breathing. Notice the natural rhythm of your breathing. You don't need to change anything; just observe. Feel the cool air entering your nose as you breathe in... and the warmth as you exhale. Let your breathing anchor you to the present moment.

Imagine you are sitting by a calm, flowing river. The water moves gently, carrying away any stress or tension you may be holding onto. With each exhale, release any worries or negative thoughts, letting the river carry them far away. If your mind starts to wander, that's okay. Simply notice the thought and gently bring your focus back to your breathing. Feel the stillness within. Each breath is a reminder of this moment,this quiet, peaceful space inside you.Take one more deep breath in... and a long exhale. Begin to bring your awareness back to the room. Slowly wiggle your fingers and toes. When you're ready, gently open your eyes. Feel calm, centered, and at peace.

Whether you realize it or not, your mind constantly works to find what you're focused on, like a magnet for the thoughts you constantly run through your mind. This can either imprison you, locking you in cycles of fear, self-doubt, and limitation, or it can free you, launching you into places of endless possibilities.

For much of my life, I allowed my mind to be a prison. I was trapped in survival mode, hyper-focused on simply making it through the day, navigating responsibilities as a young mom, enduring a toxic relationship, and coping with the weight of overwhelming loss. My thoughts were dominated by fear, scarcity, and the belief that I wasn't worthy of more. My mind found evidence to support that because that's all I looked for.

What I've learned, through the pain and struggle, is that shifting your mindset can change everything.

Once I secured a place for my children and me to live post-divorce, I had to allow myself to be present in the moment. It was something I had to work at. My mind was always ready for the other shoe to drop. I often found myself anticipating the worst. However, I kept going. With guidance, I was able to separate what was truly a threat and what was actually my imagination, fear, and scarcity mindset. From that place, I could start to view myself as empowered and capable.

Imagining the bridge my therapist at the time talked about: on one side is everything I've ever known,my past, my traumas, my insecurities, my failures. It's comfortable there because it's familiar, but it also kept me small, confined to the story I told myself about being inadequate. On the other side of the bridge is the unknown,new possibilities, growth, freedom, and abundance. But to get there, I had to cross over. Crossing that bridge requires more than action; it requires a mindset shift. It was not just about changing my situation but about changing my inner narrative.

When you decide to shift your mindset, you allow yourself to believe that the future is full of potential and that you are capable of more than what your past says you should be. It requires being intentional with your thoughts and focusing on what you want to create rather than what you want to avoid.

The Power of Focus

The mind has an incredible ability to find what it seeks. This is why you have to become deliberate about where you place your focus. If you constantly dwell on your limitations, your mind will find ways to reinforce those beliefs. But when you start focusing on your strengths, your dreams, and the possibilities ahead, your mind will work just as hard to find opportunities and pathways to make them real.

In my own journey, I had glimpses of the future I wanted. That small hope grew distant as life became more about surviving. I had to shift my mindset to move from survival mode to a place of growth. I wasn't thinking about my potential or the future I could create; I was only focused on getting through the day.

But something shifted when I started to believe that I could have more. It wasn't an overnight change but a gradual one. First, it started with curiosity. I wanted to know what it felt like to live a life that was fulfilled. I created a plan on how to get to where I wanted to be. I had to believe I was capable and begin to envision my life in a place of peace and freedom. I began to see that my pain didn't define me and that my past didn't dictate my future. I started to look for ways to grow, to heal, and to build a life that was about more than just survival. Slowly, I crossed that bridge.

The Prison of Limiting Beliefs

Your mind can either be a prison of your own beliefs, or a key to the freedom of possibilities. When you're locked in a negative mindset, it's like living in a self-imposed cell. Limiting beliefs tell you that you can't achieve your goals, that you don't deserve happiness, or that your dreams are impossible. These beliefs reinforce themselves, keeping you in a loop of doubt and fear.

One of the most challenging limiting beliefs I had to confront was the idea that I wasn't worthy of better for myself and that I wasn't capable of building a different life. I had absorbed the doubts of others, whether it was family, my ex-husband, or even society telling me what I could or couldn't do. These voices became my internal dialogue, and it took a mindset shift to realize they weren't true.

The first step in freeing yourself from these beliefs is recognizing them. What are the stories you're telling yourself that keep you from crossing that bridge? It's only when you confront those narratives that you can begin to rewrite them.

The Catalyst for Change

Once you shift your mindset, the possibilities open up. You begin to see opportunities where before there were only dead ends. Your mind, now focused on growth and potential, works in your favor rather than against you.

It wasn't until I shifted my mindset, that I began to see my challenges as stepping stones rather than barriers. Once I understood the power of my thought process, I decided to no longer view myself as a victim of my circumstances, but as someone who had the power to shape my future with the decisions I made. I realized that the things I had been through didn't make me less capable; they made me stronger, more resilient, and more determined to create a better life.

This shift allowed me to take risks I wouldn't have never taken before. It gave me the courage to start my own business, to pursue my goals in public speaking, and to write books. I went from seeing life as something happening to me, to understanding that I had the power to create my own path.

Practical Steps to Shift Your Mindset

Changing your mindset isn't about positive thinking alone, it's about being intentional in your actions and your focus. Here are some steps that helped me:

Identify Limiting Beliefs: The first step is becoming aware of the beliefs that are holding you back. Write them down, and ask yourself, "Is this true? Where did this belief come from?"

Reframe Your Narrative: Start with rewriting the story you tell yourself. Instead of focusing on what you lack or what you don't like about yourself, focus on what you have and your strengths. Shift from "I can't" to "How can I?"

Surround Yourself with Growth: Your environment plays a crucial role in your mindset. Surround yourself with people who encourage your growth and create a space that supports your new vision.

Practice Gratitude: Shifting your focus to what you're grateful for, rewires your brain to see abundance instead of scarcity.

Take Action: Mindset shifts don't work without action. Start taking small steps toward your goals. With each step your mindset will continue to evolve.

Reinventing Yourself

As life continues to move forward, we are presented with the opportunity to grow and evolve. Who you had to be to survive no longer has to be the person you present to the world. As you approach new seasons in life, adapting to your environment is necessary. Once you decide that the environment no longer serves you, there has to be a shift in your way of thinking about yourself. You have to decide, who do you want to be in the space you are growing into and then do what that person would do.

I had to suppress so many pieces of who I authentically was in order to survive. Enduring so many painful experiences as a child had cause me to lose any sense of agency over any aspect of my life. Being completely detached from my own feelings and taking on the emotions of others, had seemed to serve me well in volatile environments. Being able to anticipate the needs of others kept me perceivably safe. Pleasing people was my way to manipulate my environment to feel safe, be loved, and have control.

Once I decided that I wanted to live a fulfilling life, I had to recognize that I was giving away my power to someone else to determine my worth and value. I had to value myself and believe I was capable of achieving what I wanted for myself. My marriage defined me. My identity was so tangled with my ex-husband's expectations that I let go of any pursuit of my own will or ambition.

There was an exercise I did with my therapist, during my divorce journey, where she asked me to close my eyes and envision myself as a queen; regal and deserving of respect. It felt strange. Nothing about me felt regal. I had to learn how to view myself in a new light.

On a trip to Tennessee, I had yet another life-changing conversation. I sat next to a stranger on the flight, and we talked about life and his career the entire time. He asked me where I was headed, and he explained that he was a coach who was headed to a speaking engagement. I initially thought he coached a team of some kind, but he explained that he was a life coach. At the time, I had just been introduced to the idea of coaching while diving deep into some of my self-help gurus, such as Tony Robbins and Les Brown. The stranger advised me to read several books he recommended. He even showed me some of the frameworks he created to help others. It was a conversation that gave me more perspective about the direction of my life. He advised me to get a life coach.

As my divorce was finalized, I ended that portion of therapy. Those weekly sessions helped me get through a very difficult time. It was the place that guided me to an unfamiliar space in my life. I said goodbye to my therapist. That profound conversation with a stranger on the flight to Tennessee ignited a desire to pursue a different type of guidance, so I sought after a life coach.

One of the most moving things that stuck with me in my coaching sessions was an exercise that helped me envision who I wanted to become. We started with identifying a person that I admired as a woman and who I wanted to emulate. Who better than the powerful, elegant, and gracious, Michelle Obama. That was the type of confident assurance in myself I wanted to exude. How do I get there? I asked my coach. We went through strategies that reshaped how I viewed myself and how I embraced what I was capable of accomplishing. I developed an audacious sense of confidence I didn't know was within me. That confidence helped drive my career aspirations and my desire to serve others.

Love

I have always loved the concept of love. I really LOVE love. The warmth, the connection, the vulnerability,it all felt like the ultimate goal. But after years of pain, mistrust, and disappointment, I found myself being afraid to open up to love again. That fear didn't just shield me from heartache, it also distanced me from the very thing I actually craved, deep, meaningful connections.

There were points where I attempted to open myself up to the idea of having someone to do life with. I really wanted to find my person. However, fear crept into potential relationships. I became avoidant, unwilling to let anyone get too close. I longed for intimacy yet pushed it away, sabotaging opportunities for love before they had the chance to blossom. More often than not, I sought out emotionally unavailable people, a way to validate my belief that I was unworthy of being truly loved. It was as if I was creating scenarios where rejection and disappointment were inevitable, confirming my internal story that I was unwanted.

But as I began to reinvent myself in other areas of life, I realized that this pattern wasn't serving me. The walls I built for protection became my prison, isolating me from the love and trust I yearned for. I had to understand that love wasn't my enemy, fear was. Fear of being vulnerable, of being hurt, of losing control. Once I recognized that, I continued to reframe the narrative I created about myself.

The journey toward future love requires a new level of self-awareness. I had to become in tune with who I was beyond the survival mode that had dominated my thinking for so long. Being in survival mode meant staying disconnected from my emotions, numbing myself to protect against future pain. But in doing so, I also blocked out true connection and love.

I realized I had to let go of the belief that I had to shield myself from love to avoid heartbreak. Instead, I have learned to embrace the truth that love, with all its risks, is a vital part of living fully. To trust again, I had to first trust myself; trust that

I was worthy of love, and that even if I got hurt, I have the strength to heal and grow from it.

One of the greatest sources of healing came from reconnecting with people who knew me, my childhood friends and family. They weren't just familiar faces; they were reminders of who I was when I was open and free before the life I chose made me cautious about being hurt. Together, we embarked on adventures, creating a new environment that was filled with love, support, and community.

Through these relationships, I began to feel safe enough to let my guard down. These connections taught me that love isn't just romantic, it can also be the bonds we form with people who lift us up and accept us for who we are.

Friendships are the vitality of life. It makes the journey all the more exciting. One of the most spiritual encounters I had was traveling with my closest friend—soaking in the awe of God's creation and truly enjoying all that life has to offer.

True friendship is where you can just be. It's a sacred space where masks come off, and you're free to expose the most vulnerable pieces of yourself without fear of judgment. In a world that often demands performance,where we feel pressured to meet expectations, be productive, or act a certain way, friendship becomes a sanctuary of authenticity.

In true friendship, you don't have to perform. You don't have to meet any standard beyond showing up with empathy, understanding, and the willingness to listen. It's a relationship that thrives on mutual respect and emotional safety. You know you are loved not for what you can do, but for who you are at your core. This kind of friendship allows you to strip away the layers of armor that protect you from the outside world. It's where you can exhale.

For me, my friendships were vital in my journey of learning to trust again. I had been so used to protecting myself, to keeping people at arm's length for fear that they would confirm my deepest fears, that I wasn't enough or wasn't wanted. But in the company of true friends, I was reminded that I didn't have to constantly be on guard. I could be vulnerable, share my pain, my dreams, and even my insecurities, and still be met with love.

This kind of friendship is rooted in the daily acts of showing up, of giving space for someone to fully be themselves. From that foundation, I realized that building romantic relationships should also come from that place of authenticity. The beauty of true friendship is that it becomes a model for all other relationships; relationships that allow you to grow, to heal, and to be seen as you are, not as you think you should be.

My connection to my cousins is something that is just as important now that we have grown up. We share some of the same experiences and dealt with the same struggles; creating a bond that is unshakable. With them, I don't have to explain myself, they already know. Whether we're laughing at old memories, comforting each other through hard times, or sharing some hard truths, I know I have a place where I will always feel seen, valued, and protected.

In a world where relationships can sometimes feel transactional or fragile, my cousins remind me what unconditional love looks like. They have been my mirrors, reflecting the strength I sometimes forgot I had, and they have been my shield, stepping in to protect me when I couldn't protect myself. That sense of safety isn't just a childhood memory, it's a foundation that still supports me as I navigate life and relationships. It reminds me that true connection, whether with family, friends, or a partner, should always leave you feeling loved and safe.

Surround yourself with people who make you want to be your best self. Friendships also hold you accountable. Accountable for the things you say you want to accomplish. Accountable to the growth you want to maintain. Having people in your life who will keep it real in a way that isn't damaging, but inspirational, will help you achieve your goals. We aren't meant to be alone. Even in the Bible, God said, "It is not good for man to be alone" (Genesis 2:18). We were created to be relational, to connect with others on deeper levels. It's woven into our DNA, part of the very essence of who we are as human beings. Our relationships, whether platonic or romantic, are mirrors reflecting not only our current state, but where we're heading in life.

The key isn't just to connect with anyone, it's to seek out relationships that are healthy, nurturing, and aligned with your purpose. So many of us, myself included, have fallen into patterns of attracting or holding on to emotionally unavailable people, often without even realizing that it's rooted in how we see ourselves. We accept what we think we deserve, which is why a mindset shift is crucial before we enter into new relationships.

You have to ask yourself, "Am I building relationships that support where I'm going? Or am I repeating old patterns that keep me stuck in places I no longer belong?" When I realized this, I knew I needed to shift from a survival mindset that had me out of touch with my emotions. It was time to embrace vulnerability, to allow love into my life again, and to be open to the possibility of being hurt, but also to the possibility of experiencing the fullness of love.

Reflective Questions:

What beliefs about love are you holding onto? How are they shaping your relationships?

What fears keep you from being vulnerable and open to love? How can you start trusting yourself and others more in your relationships?

Who are the people in your life that remind you of who you truly are, and how can you nurture those connections? Following the petals:

Identify Patterns – Reflect on past relationships and identify any patterns where you may have sabotaged love or sought out emotionally unavailable partners. Write down how those patterns served your fear and why it's time to let them go.

Learn to Embrace Vulnerability – Take small steps toward vulnerability, whether it's opening up more in your current relationships or allowing someone new to see the real you. Practice being honest with your emotions without fearing the outcome.

Surround Yourself with Supportive People – Spend time with your friends and loved ones who make you feel safe and loved. Let these relationships remind you that love can be a source of strength, not pain.

Self-Compassion – Be kind to yourself through the process. Healing your relationship with love takes time. Practice self-compassion by acknowledging your fears while also reassuring yourself that you are worthy of deep and meaningful love.

TRUE FRIENDSHIP IS WHERE YOU CAN JUST BE. IT'S A SACRED SPACE WHERE MASKS COME OFF, AND YOU'RE FREE TO EXPOSE THE MOST VULNERABLE PIECES OF YOURSELF WITHOUT FEAR OF JUDGMENT. IN A WORLD THAT OFTEN DEMANDS PERFORMANCE—WHERE WE FEEL PRESSURED TO MEET EXPECTATIONS, BE PRODUCTIVE, OR ACT A CERTAIN WAY— FRIENDSHIP BECOMES A SANCTUARY OF AUTHENTICITY.

Know Thyself

What I love about the philosophy of self-examination, historically discussed by the great Socrates, is that it calls us to be curious enough about life. Curious enough to question our values, assumptions, perspectives, motivations, and purpose. The journey of understanding this is a lifelong commitment to yourself. In pursuing this life of curiosity, I have come to gain a better understanding of how I interact with the world around me.

For so long I cruised through life on autopilot, shaped by my experiences, trauma, and fear. To know myself was the process I needed to start for me to experience transformation. In accepting certain narratives about myself, I adopted beliefs that limited my perspective on who I was, forming barriers to what was possible for my life. Removing those constraints through questioning my belief system, allowed me to experience freedom.

Reacting to fear was a natural response to everything. Being able to pause and ask myself difficult questions to reveal deeper understanding: Why do I believe this? What evidence do I have for this belief? How is this belief serving or limiting me? I had used this process to slow down and respond to stressful situations as I grew toward self-reinvention.

Limiting beliefs come from societal expectations, internalized fears, or trauma. Going unchecked, these beliefs prevent us from activating our fullest potential. Asking the right questions can reveal the foundation of those beliefs, extract the narrative, revamp it, and replace it with a new truth that empowers us.

In small, undetectable ways, those limiting beliefs whispered feelings of inadequacies to my soul. Those whispers manifested in ways that kept me small; swallowed by the beliefs that I wasn't capable, worthy, or deserving of anything that looked like love or success. Those beliefs defined me, forcing me to accept that I had to settle for less because of my past mistakes and misfortune. When I learned to reflect on and question those ideas, I've come to understand which part of the narrative is a lie. I continue to remind myself of that. The whispers try to come back at times, but I have the tools to identify them, allowing me to recall a new narrative to counter those intrusive thoughts; it is an ongoing process.

Imagine the heaviness of confronting the darkest parts of ourselves; it's much like the muddy waters the lotus must move through to blossom. The journey to a more intentional and meaningful life is not easy. It is a road that is challenging, uncomfortable, and scary. But remember, the unfamiliar path leads to truth, wisdom, and freedom. Freedom to live with purpose and possibility.

No matter where you are in life, if there is an inkling of curiosity that there could be more for you, it comes to you because there is more. More life, more peace, more joy. Do not let your current circumstances make you lose sight of what is possible. Moving forward can be painful. It can feel like a loss. It is uncomfortable, but on the other side of the bridge, is hope, relentless hope. It waits for you with open arms, ready to lead you into the fullness of life that you've always deserved. Trust that, take the step, and never look back.

The Lotus Foundation INC

My mom has always had a resounding desire to give back. Her generosity and willingness to help others have always been admirable. Watching her give freely, without expecting anything in return, planted a seed in me—a deep desire to create meaningful, selfless pathways for those seeking guidance.

For my mom, that passion centered around helping single mothers. It was a calling so strong that, at times, it felt overwhelming. Yet, as life unfolded and responsibilities grew heavier, she was reluctantly forced to place her dream on hold. Watching her press pause on something so close to her heart sparked a fire in me—a determination to one day help her bring that vision to life.

As I drew closer to my own purpose, something beautiful happened: I began to connect with my mom in a deeper, more profound way. That connection led us to unite our shared passions and give birth to something greater than ourselves — The Lotus Foundation INC.

The Lotus Foundation INC is a nonprofit organization dedicated to empowering single mothers by breaking the cycle of poverty and fostering self-sustainability. Through mental health wellness, educational scholarships, career planning, and comprehensive resources, TLF equips single mothers with the tools and opportunities needed to achieve economic independence, create brighter futures for their families, and inspire generational change.

Appreciation

It is my community that has given me the courage to share my story. It is the love and support from my friends and family that give me strength to be great. I could not muster up the motivation to complete this on my own. I am only as great as the circle of amazing people that surround me.

Mom: Thank you for all the sacrifices you made to make sure I had exposure to what was possible for me. I appreciate the example of kindness, class, and determination. You are my first example of love.

Dad: Thank you for teaching me about life. Your guidance and demonstration of love gave me the greatest foundation. It took me a while, but I came back to what you taught me.

My cousins -Jean Douglas, Robert Webster: You are my safe place. Thank you for being my biggest support. Jean, you have opened doors for me that have changed my life and I am eternally grateful. Robert, you are the consistent picture of protection, love and support.

Lynda Wheeler: You are my living, breathing diary. The kind of support the greatest friendships are made of. Thank you for the adventures, and for being my biggest hype woman!

I've had three therapists who transformed my life in ways which words cannot express my gratitude. Each one a pivotal piece in my journey, at different stages. One helped me see myself as smart and capable. She helped me through grief and equipped me with tools to survive. The next guided me to safety, helping me awaken from the trance of hopelessness. The third helped me rewrite the narrative I had about myself. He has given me tools to exit the survival mode and enter into thriving as an individual.

Notes

Murky Waters
The Avengers. Directed by Joss Whedon, performances by Robert Downey Jr., Chris Evans, and Scarlett Johansson, Marvel Studios, 2012.
☐ Used to draw a parallel between the narrator's former spouse's emotional volatility and the character of the Hulk, who is always angry beneath the surface—highlighting suppressed rage in abusive relationships.

Bipolar
Kolkey, Jeff. "Violent Crime Up in Rockford, but Crime Down Overall." Rockford Register Star, May 17, 2014.
☐ Used to highlight the context of growing up in a high-crime area, shaping stress responses and constant hypervigilance in adolescence.

Mom
National Coalition Against Domestic Violence (NCADV). "Domestic Violence Statistics."
☐ Supports the depiction of family instability and intergenerational trauma, particularly in the mother-child dynamic.

Fight Flight Freeze
Family Guy. Created by Seth MacFarlane, Fox, 1999–present.
☐ Referenced to illustrate how humor and media provided both emotional escape and subtle reflections of dysfunction, shaping early coping mechanisms.

Giedd, J. N. "Structural Magnetic Resonance Imaging of the Adolescent Brain." Annals of the New York Academy of Sciences, 2004.
☐ Explains the continued brain development during adolescence, especially the prefrontal cortex, relating to impulsive behavior and emotional control.

Perry, Bruce D. The Boy Who Was Raised as a Dog. Basic

Books, 2006.
☐ Offers a framework for understanding how trauma alters a child's ability to form secure attachments and regulate emotion.

National Child Traumatic Stress Network (NCTSN). "The Effects of Trauma on the Brain Development of Children."
☐ Reinforces how trauma during critical periods shapes brain structure and behavior, especially around safety, trust, and threat response.

Harvard University Center on the Developing Child. "Key Concepts: Toxic Stress."
☐ Provides evidence of how chronic exposure to toxic stress impacts long-term health, decision-making, and relational capacity.

Transform and Transcend
Ruiz, Don Miguel. The Four Agreements: A Practical Guide to Personal Freedom. Amber-Allen Publishing, 1997.
☐ Tied to healing and personal growth through self-awareness and behavioral transformation, this work supports the chapter's themes of breaking mental patterns and embracing a new narrative.

Mindset Shift
Perry, Bruce D., & Winfrey, Oprah. What Happened to You?: Conversations on Trauma, Resilience, and Healing. Flatiron Books, 2021.
☐ Explores trauma-informed healing and mindset evolution after adversity, offering a compassionate lens for reframing personal experiences.

Van Der Kolk, Bessel A. The Body Keeps the Score. Viking, 2014.
☐ Details the physiological and psychological effects of trauma and methods for recovery, validating the mind-body connection described in the chapter.

Know Thyself

Socrates. "Know thyself." Classical Greek aphorism, attributed through historical references to the Oracle of Delphi.
☐ Underscores self-inquiry and reflection as essential tools for personal growth and healing, resonating with the chapter's emphasis on introspection and identity.

Explains the long-term effects of chronic stress and trauma on the brain. Available at: www.developingchild.harvard.edu

Pathways and Resources

Domestic Violence Resources

National Domestic Violence Hotline Website: www.thehotline.org
Phone: 1-800-799-SAFE (7233)
Text: Text "START" to 88788
Services: 24/7 support for survivors, safety planning, and access to local resources.

RAINN (Rape, Abuse & Incest National Network) Website: www.rainn.org
Phone: 1-800-656-HOPE (4673)
Services: Support for sexual assault survivors, including chat hotlines and local resource directories.

Futures Without Violence
Website: www.futureswithoutviolence.org
Services: Training, advocacy, and educational materials for survivors and professionals.

Love Is Respect (for teens and young adults) Website: www.loveisrespect.org
Phone: 1-866-331-9474
Text: Text "LOVEIS" to 22522
Services: Focused on dating abuse prevention and support.

StrongHearts Native Helpline
Website: www.strongheartshelpline.org Phone: 1-844-7NATIVE (1-844-762-8483)
Services: Culturally appropriate support for Native American and Alaska Native survivors.

Mental Health Resources

National Suicide Prevention Lifeline (now 988 Suicide & Crisis Lifeline) Website: www.988lifeline.org

Phone: Dial 988
Services: 24/7 crisis support and suicide prevention.

Substance Abuse and Mental Health Services Administration (SAMH- SA)
Website: www.samhsa.gov Phone: 1-800-662-HELP (4357)
Services: Free, confidential treatment referrals and information.

National Alliance on Mental Illness (NAMI) Website: www.nami.org
Phone: 1-800-950-NAMI (6264) or text "HELPLINE" to 62640
Services: Mental health advocacy, education, and support groups.

Crisis Text Line
Website: www.crisistextline.org Text: Text "HOME" to 741741
Services: Free, 24/7 crisis counseling via text.

Therapy for Black Girls
Website: www.therapyforblackgirls.com
Services: Therapist directories and mental health resources specifically for Black women.

The Trevor Project (LGBTQ+ youth support) Website: www.thetrevorproject.org
Phone: 1-866-488-7386
Text/Chat: Available on their website
Services: Crisis support and mental health resources for LGBTQ+ youth.

Housing Resources

National Coalition for the Homeless Website: www.national-homeless.org
Services: Advocacy, education, and connections to local housing support.

HUD Exchange (U.S. Department of Housing and Urban Development) Website: www.hud.gov/program_offices/comm_planning/homeless Services: Emergency housing assistance, Section 8 vouchers, and home- lessness prevention.

National Alliance to End Homelessness Website: www.end-homelessness.org
Services: Advocacy and policy recommendations for addressing home- lessness.

Domestic Shelters
Website: www.domesticshelters.org
Services: Searchable database of shelters and housing for domestic violence survivors.

Catholic Charities USA
Website: www.catholiccharitiesusa.org
Services: Housing assistance, shelters, and social services for individuals and families in crisis.
ShelterSafe (Canada) Website: www.sheltersafe.ca
Services: Searchable directory of shelters for women in Canada.

Low-Income Housing Guide Website: www.lowincomehousing.us
Services: Affordable housing directories and emergency housing resources.

TO FIND OUT MORE ABOUT THE FOUNDATION VISIT

THE-LOTUS-FOUNDATION.COM

www.ingramcontent.com/pod-product-compliance
Lightning Source LLC
Chambersburg PA
CBHW051149120626
46547CB00012B/1008